STYLISHLY
DRAWN

STYLISHLY
DRAWN

CONTEMPORARY

FASHION

ILLUSTRATION

LAIRD BORRELLI

HARRY N. ABRAMS, INC., PUBLISHERS

Library of Congress Cataloging-in-Publication Data

Borrelli, Laird
    Stylishly drawn : contemporary fashion illustration / by Laird Borrelli
        p.   cm.
    ISBN 0–8109–4122–8
    1. Fashion drawing.   I. Title
TT509.B67 2000
741.6'72—dc21   00-38107

Published in 2000 by Harry N. Abrams, Incorporated, New York

Printed and bound in Italy

 Harry N. Abrams, Inc.
100 Fifth Avenue
New York, N.Y. 10011
www.abramsbooks.com

page 1
JORDI LABANDA
Hussein Chalayan
Gouache on paper
AB Magazine, June 1998

pages 2-3
ANJA KROENCKE
Mixed media on paper
Madame Figaro
9 October 1999

page 4
TANYA LING
Dries Van Noten
Mixed media on paper
Joyce (Hong Kong)
Summer 1999

CONTENTS

INTRODUCTION

Fashion Illustration Now stands as witness to the unparalleled variety of fashion illustration today. Each of the twenty-nine illustrators featured has contributed to the blossoming of a métier that was considered, until recently, to be endangered.

The decline of fashion illustration can be traced back to the late 1930s when *Vogue* began to replace its celebrated illustrated covers with photographic ones and the dark room took precedence over the drawing board. The preference for photography over illustration became most marked in the 1950s, however. Kenneth Paul Block, an illustrator who began his career then, states simply: 'I started doing something at the end of its history.' The journalist, Sonia Rachline, attributes this shift in interest from illustration to photography to a sea change in the fashion industry. Specifically, emphasis started to shift from haute couture, which had always encouraged collaborations between artists and designers (Salvador Dalí and Elsa Schiaparelli, for example), towards technology and

Sometimes you're an art movement

JEAN-PHILIPPE DELHOMME
'Sometimes you're an art movement' (Givenchy). Gouache on paper. Advertisement, 1993
Courtesy of Barneys New York

machine-sewn (profit-making) prêt-à-porter. Fashion illustration began to be regarded as precious and recherché rather than contemporary in comparison to photography. As Rachline explains: 'on ne veut pas de l'art, on veut du réalisme', that is, photography's 'reality'. Gradually art directors, who had for years accounted for illustration as a standard and expected means of fashion presentation, left little if any room for illustration in their layouts (with a few exceptions, notably for the Puerto Rican-born illustrator Antonio). From the 1960s to the 1980s, fashion illustration was in decline. Only after that did illustration begin to enter a period of renaissance that is now burgeoning. As New York illustrator Tobie Giddio said in a 1999 interview: 'it's a boom time for illustration'.

To best understand what is happening in illustration today, let's return to the 1980s and early 1990s when the 'boom time' took root. This was when several magazines began to showcase illustration, most notably *Vanity* from Italy, featuring covers by François Berthoud; *La Mode en Peinture* from France; as well as *Interview* and *Details* from New York, the former featuring illustrated fashion editorials and the latter end pages by Ruben Toledo. Additionally, illustrated advertisements began to reappear. The most influential of these were Jean-Philippe Delhomme's for Barneys New York, the cutting-edge retailer.

Jodie Shields, a journalist writing in *Vogue* in 1994, asserts that: 'by all accounts [Barneys] gets the credit for pioneering illustration's current comeback'. Its groundbreaking series of advertisements was launched in 1993 and ran through 1996. Delhomme's illustrations were paired with witty copy by Glenn O'Brien – 'Sometimes you call Brooklyn the left bank', or 'Fiona thought self-service was the story of Victor's life.' Precisely *because* they were illustrated, Barneys' advertisements managed to seem both reassuringly old-fashioned and entirely new. After being absent, even *démodé*, for so long, fashion illustration now seemed contemporary and 'edgy again but in a familiar, handcrafted way. Moreover, Delhomme's ads for Barneys were the antithesis of the airbrushed perfection of supermodel and celebrity endorsements. They were painted in gouache with his signature soft, squiggly line and the characters and clothes depicted were vague and ambiguous. Yet, quite surrealistically, the clothing, hair styling and perfume credits were provided in the copy.

The Barneys campaign was soft sell. It was droll. People were able to insert themselves into the ads – which they did, writing in to say that they identified with Delhomme's characters. At the same time fashion was changing: the romantic, greenhouse appeal of boutique fashion was challenged by the street. Suddenly supermodels were superseded by waifs and grunge rocked the

PIET PARIS
Mixed media on paper
Man, July 1998

fashion world for at least fifteen minutes. Calvin Klein launched cK, a unisex fragrance advertised by 'real' people. The fashion equivalent of the unisex fragrance was the minimal, androgynous silhouette.

The photographic images that accompanied these changes in fashion were gritty and 'in your face', the complete antithesis of Delhomme's ads. They were transgressive rather than ambiguous, trippy rather than dreamy. This style of photography, Nan Goldin lite, became known as 'heroin-chic'. It created a buzz and sparked outrage. 'The pop culture cutting edge', wrote Kurt Anderson in *The New Yorker*, 'has been [defined by] a mass-market explicitness… Don't go there? We're there.' Heroin-chic's explicit images were first published in such magazines as *The Face,* which itself was challenging traditional conventions of appropriateness, beauty, and modes of fashion presentation.

The late 1990s were a period of repositioning. Fashion careened between space-age minimalism and retro-centred decadence, zen-like restraint and lavish embellishment. The appeal of retro might be escapist, away from the explicit, but it can also be explained as a typical millennial review of the past. At the *fin de siècle* there was a proliferation of magazines, web sites, zines and other new media. Because of the number of titles available and vast Internet resources, it was difficult for a new publication or site to stand out. It was also a challenge for photography to keep up and to look new. Consequently, new titles began using illustration to distinguish themselves.

Many of the publications using fashion illustration were not, in industry terms, 'fashion books', rather they were 'shelter' books, like Wallpaper*, in which fashion is covered as an extension of design and lifestyle. When Steven LaGuardia, creative director of the Louis, Boston store, was asked to identify 'the next big thing' by *WWD*, he responded: 'magazines [that] are moving to be more lifestyle and attitude-based, rather than gender-based'. (This emphasis on fashionable living has been literally taken up by fashion designers, many of whom are branching out into housewares.) Ironically, traditionally female fashion magazines, such as *Vogue* and *Harper's Bazaar,* usually relegate illustration to non-editorial spots, most often the horoscope page.

JASON BROOKS Macintosh, Adobe Photoshop. German *Elle*, 1998

Wallpaper* is a design magazine with the tag line: 'the stuff that surrounds you'. It has, to some extent, pioneered the current revival of illustration. Richard Spenser Powell, a designer at *Wallpaper**, considers illustration to be an 'extension of fashion and what it can show'. Yet, according to Donald Schneider, art director of *Paris Vogue*, photography provides a sort of 'reader service' in a fashion magazine – people want to see actual garments (despite the many ways that a photograph can be manipulated, it is still considered to be 'real'.)

Yet if it is an attitude or style that needs to be expressed, illustration is an equally effective means of communication. And because it has been so long neglected, illustration seems fresh, as if it were a 'new way of presentation', says Spenser Powell, who adds that the reader response has been extremely positive. Now new titles – *Nylon, Citizen K International* and *Vogue Nippon* – are actively commissioning illustrators. In fact, illustration is sometimes being used, according to Delhomme, 'as a *bizarre* [quaint]

alternative to fashion photography'. Fashion illustration is an art unto itself. It is a métier with its own (evolving) history, conventions and commercial applications. 'An illustrator, not unlike a fine artist', says Giddio, 'can create a vast range of work, from the most classic elegant drawings to the most abstracted deconstructed forms' (as she does herself).

The artists featured in *Fashion Illustration Now* work in a variety of styles. In fact, not all of them define themselves as fashion illustrators. Ruben Toledo doesn't define himself this way, nor does Delhomme, who Shields quotes as saying: 'I never claimed to be a fashion illustrator. It's people that interest me.' And Jeffrey Fulvimari defines himself as a 'commercial illustrator' whose characters are 'sometimes used in fashion situations'. What then is the definition of a contemporary fashion illustrator, or of contemporary fashion illustration? It is a question that I have been asked over and over again in the course of writing this book.

Fashion illustration is primarily about clothes, but as Mats Gustafson has said, it is not just 'about the tissue'. Unlike a fashion plate, a contemporary fashion illustration is more than a 'costume portrait' (partly because photography can show clothes in detail). A fashion illustration captures the posture and the air, the attitude and the mood of a clothed figure, alone or in a fashionable setting or situation. It does this explicitly or suggestively. A fashion illustration is evocative. And even if it is not visibly so, it is self-conscious. A contemporary fashion illustration often references – or reacts to – the history of fashion presentation, both words and images. Fashion is, after all, a romantic fiction that astonishes, charms and tempts us.

In *Fashion Illustration Now*, artists are divided stylistically into three broad groups: 'Sensualists'; 'Gamines & Sophisticates'; and 'Technocrats'. Each of these categories is more fully defined at the opening of each chapter. In brief, the Sensualists – Ruben Alterio, François Berthoud, Tobie Giddio, Mats Gustafson, Kareem Iliya, Tanya Ling, Lorenzo Mattotti, Piet Paris, Hiroshi Tanabe and Ruben Toledo – work in the fine-arts tradition with paints, inks, linocuts and stencils. The process of making the illustration is as important to these artists as is the subject.

The second section, Gamines & Sophisticates, features artists whose work is figurative and who use caricature and aspects of cartooning to create characters and to comment on behaviour. As Robert Clyde Anderson says of his work: 'I hope it conveys a bit of my own attitude about this whole world of fashion and style – that it's fun and stimulating and fascinating but it takes itself a bit too seriously some of the time.' The artists included in this chapter are: Robert Clyde Anderson, Carlotta, Amy Davis, Jean-Philippe

JEAN-PHILIPPE DELHOMME
Comme des Garçons
Men's show, Paris
Gouache on paper
Artist's collection, 1998

Delhomme, Jeffrey Fulvimari, Kiraz, Anja Kroencke, Jordi Labanda, Demetrios Psillos, Maurice Vellekoop and Liselotte Watkins.

Fashion Illustration Now also includes the newest style of illustration, computer-generated art. Computer artists, or Technocrats, usually start with a drawing, but manipulate and transform their work beyond their initial sketch on the computer. Even illustrators who prefer more traditional media recognize computer technology as illustration's newest frontier. Computer-ready art is easy to use and to transmit globally. And, as Donald Schneider told me in an interview, the computer 'eliminates all excuses'. Artwork can be re-coloured or re-sized at the touch of a button. The Technocrats – Jason Brooks, Michael Economy, Yoko Ikeno, Maxine Law, Thierry Perez, Graham Rounthwaite, Kristian Russell and Ed. Tsuwaki – find inspiration in sources as diverse as Matisse and The Matrix, Japanimation and Pop Art. As a group, their work is distinguished by the technological means by which it is made. Surprisingly, perhaps, an interest in fashion and technology links the work of the Technocrats to an early antecedent, the fashion plate, which was also mechanically produced.

Part of the appeal of contemporary fashion illustration is its status as an art. As many of the illustrators in *Fashion Illustration Now* have acknowledged, people yearn for what is personal. Whether drawn on paper or done in Photoshop or Illustrator, fashion illustration shows the presence of the hand, which can be comforting, especially in what Glenn O'Brien describes as our '100-channel, 24 hour-a-day, celebrity world'. In addition, fashion illustrators create fantasies. In the end, a fashion illustration is truly, in Schneider's words, 'a visual luxury'.

MATS GUSTAFSON
Romeo Gigli
Watercolour and ink on paper
Artwork commissioned by the designer, 1990

RUBEN **ALTERIO** FRANÇOIS **BERTHOUD** TOBIE **GIDDIO** MATS **GUSTAFSON** KAREEM **ILIYA**
TANYA **LING** LORENZO **MATTOTTI** PIET **PARIS** HIROSHI **TANABE** RUBEN **TOLEDO**

PART ONE
THE SENSUALISTS

Paints and inks, papers, colours and textures are the protagonists of Sensualist illustrations. The role of the Sensualist illustrator is to be strong and silent, like a *deus ex machina*. Part of the appeal of this style is the silent, but palpable, presence of the artist, which is subtly revealed by the languorous trace of a brush or the jagged mark of a woodblock, expressing both skill and labour.

Sensualists delight in the materials and techniques of their profession, exploring the capabilities of their media. The work of the ten artists included in this section is diverse, ranging from the impressionistic to the graphic.

Fluidity and transparency relate the work of Mats Gustafson, Kareem Iliya and Ruben Alterio. Gustafson's preferred media are watercolour and ink, which he applies in transparent veils of colour that seem to lap one against the other. His watercolour drawings are distinguished by their superfluidity and lightness. Iliya works in the same media, but uses saturated fields of bright colour that burst and radiate around white space. Alterio prefers a more sombre 'renaissance' palette, creating multi-layered illustrations with turpentine-tempered oil paints.

In contrast, Tobie Giddio explores the dramatic juxtaposition of the transparent and the opaque. She combines ink with watercolours or translucent coloured films, almost as if she were setting coloured glass into lead panes. At the other extreme is Lorenzo Mattotti, who uses oil acrylics that are entirely opaque and viscous.

François Berthoud, Piet Paris and Hiroshi Tanabe use mechanical means to create their fashion illustrations. Berthoud's striking images are often made with linocuts. The marks or *griffes* of the carved blocks impressed on the paper are raw and provocative. Berthoud's technique also recalls early methods used in making fashion plates, which were mechanically reproduced using woodcuts and engravings, followed by hand-coloured lithographs and photographic processes. Tanabe works in ink and then manipulates his images via low-tech methods so that although his work is drawn, it has the appearance of a woodblock print. Paris also starts with a drawing, but then creates precise stencils. Following that he cuts out and paints or colours these with a roller.

Tanya Ling and Ruben Toledo work in a more figurative style than that of the other Sensualists. Toledo's witty figures are drawn in a sharp calligraphic style in ink, while Ling's lyrical ladies are created with mixed media, including pen, ink, acrylics, make-up and even glitter.

RUBEN ALTERIO

A painter and illustrator, Ruben Alterio works in a quick and impressionistic style. His concern is with atmosphere, silhouette and movement. With rich Renaissance colours, he captures 'sol y sombra' (sun and shadow) with voluptuous brushstrokes.

RIGHT
Hervé Leger
Oil and turpentine on paper
Neiman Marcus Advertising Campaign, 1997

OPPOSITE
Guy Laroche
Oil and turpentine on paper
Neiman Marcus Advertising Campaign, 1997

RUBEN ALTERIO
ABOVE
Donna Karan Collection
Oil and turpentine on paper
Neiman Marcus Advertising Campaign, 1997

OPPOSITE
Thierry Mugler
Oil and turpentine on paper
Neiman Marcus Advertising Campaign, 1997

FRANÇOIS BERTHOUD

François Berthoud uses printing techniques, especially linocuts, which he customizes to match his ideas. He likes to mix popular and classic culture to communicate 'beauty, elegance and style' – with humour. Accoring to Berthoud, illustration is not in competition to photography; rather it is 'another language and therefore it tells other stories'.

Gucci
Monotype, oil on paper
Amica, 1998

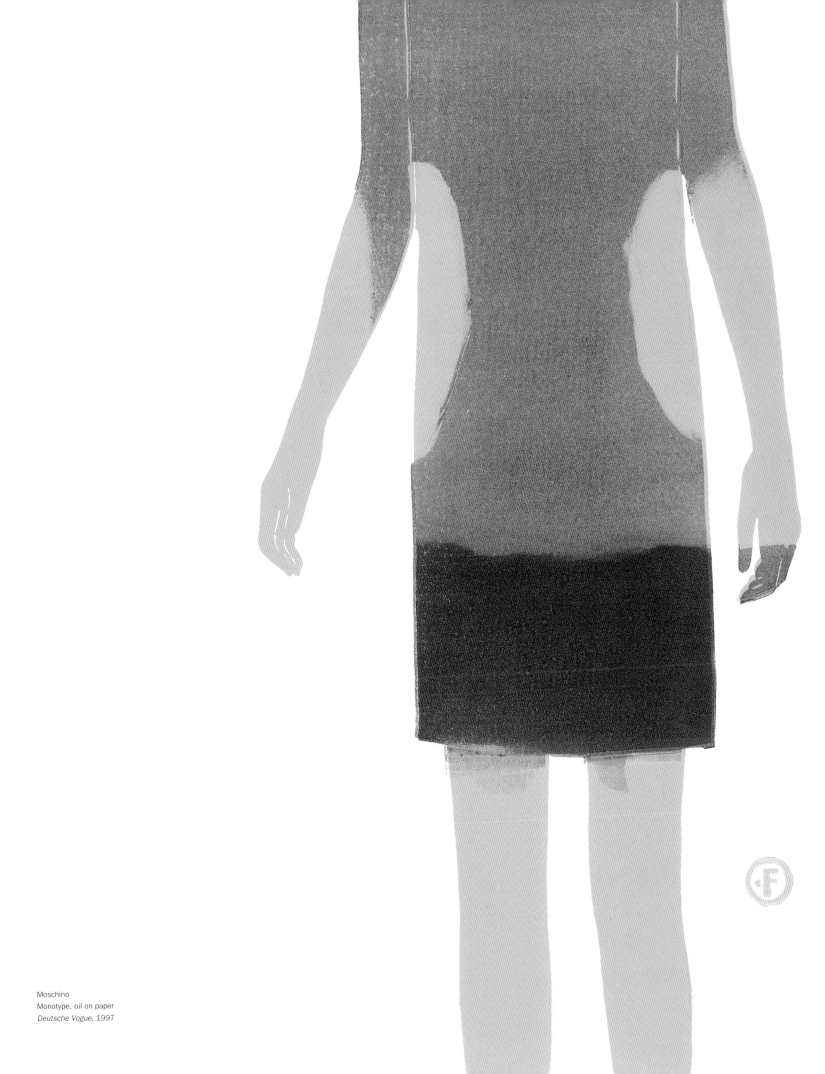

Moschino
Monotype, oil on paper
Deutsche Vogue, 1997

FRANÇOIS BERTHOUD
Alexander McQueen
Monotype, oil on paper
Vogue Italia, 1998

OPPOSITE
Versace Couture
Monotype, oil on paper
Amica, 1998

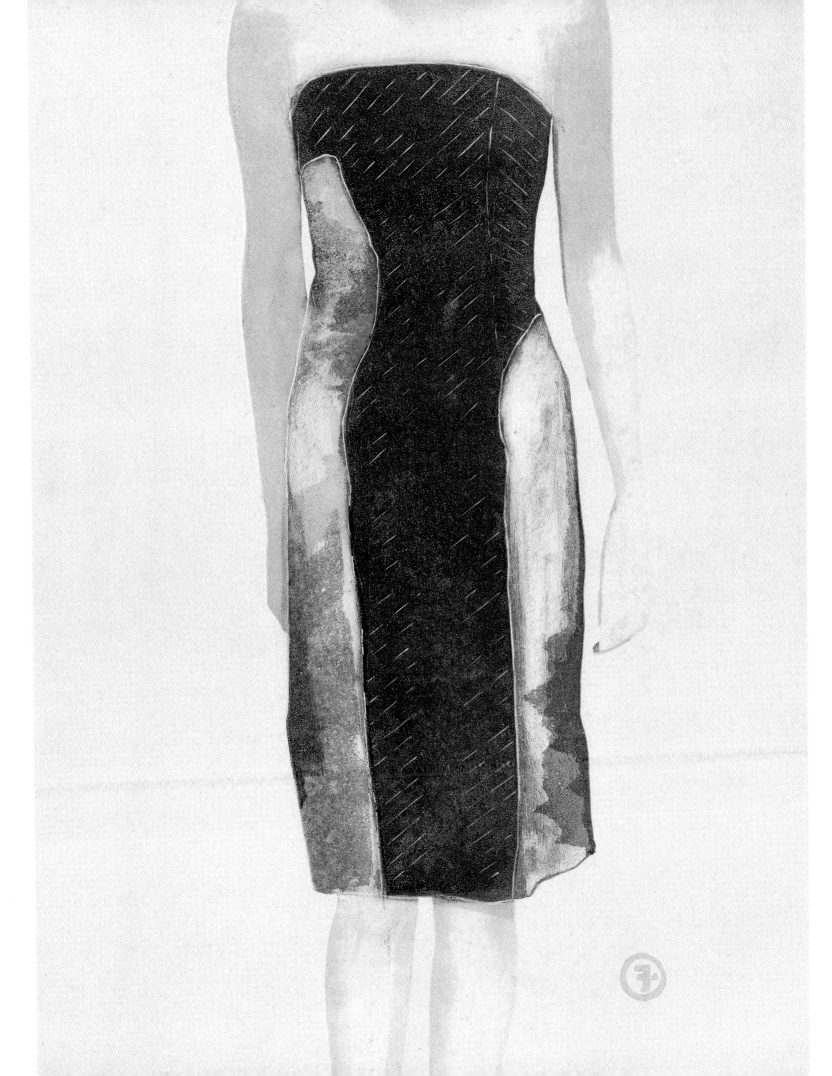

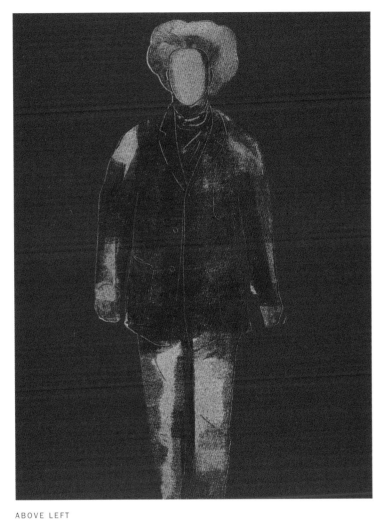

ABOVE LEFT
Comme des Garçons
Monotype, oil on paper
L'Uomo Vogue, 1998

ABOVE RIGHT
Martin Sitbon
Monotype, oil on paper
Visionaire, 1998

OPPOSITE
Christian Lacroix
Monotype, oil on paper
Detour, 1999

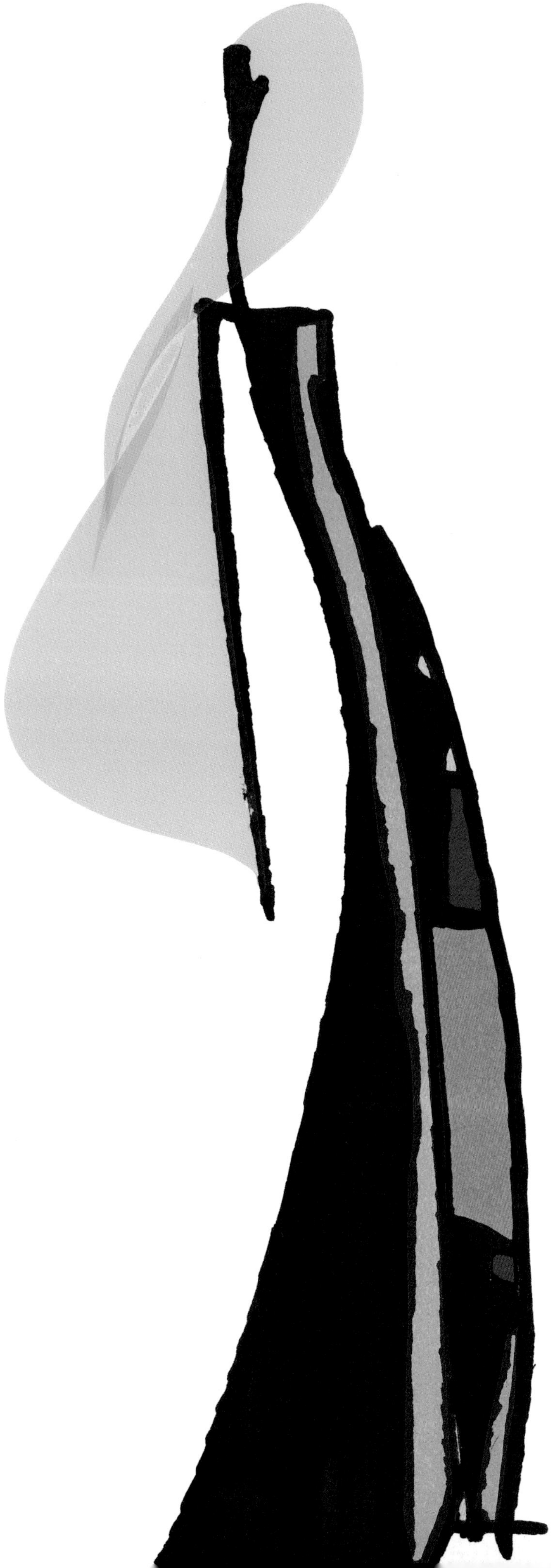

TOBIE GIDDIO

Elegantly clad and formally posed, Giddio's abstract and organic figures are created with Sumi ink, watercolours and Pantone films. Giddio describes her work as being 'very internal and beyond the surface'.

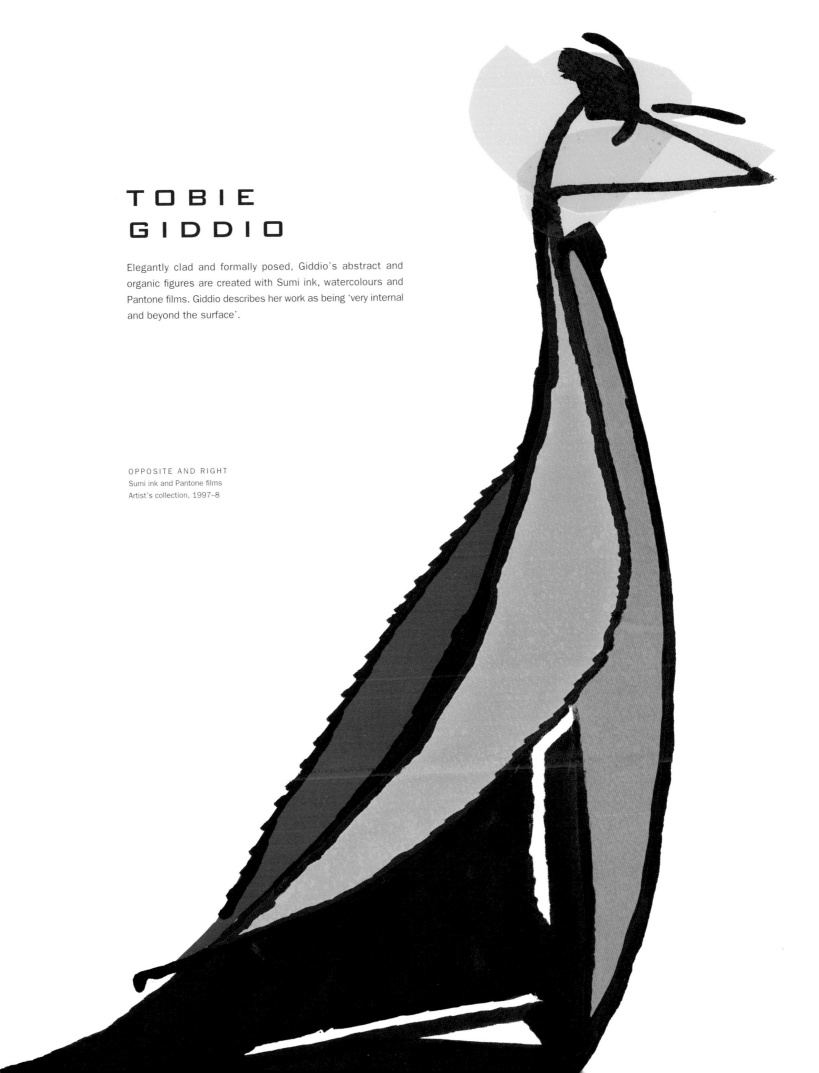

RIGHT AND OPPOSITE
Sumi ink and Pantone films
Artist's collection, 1997–8

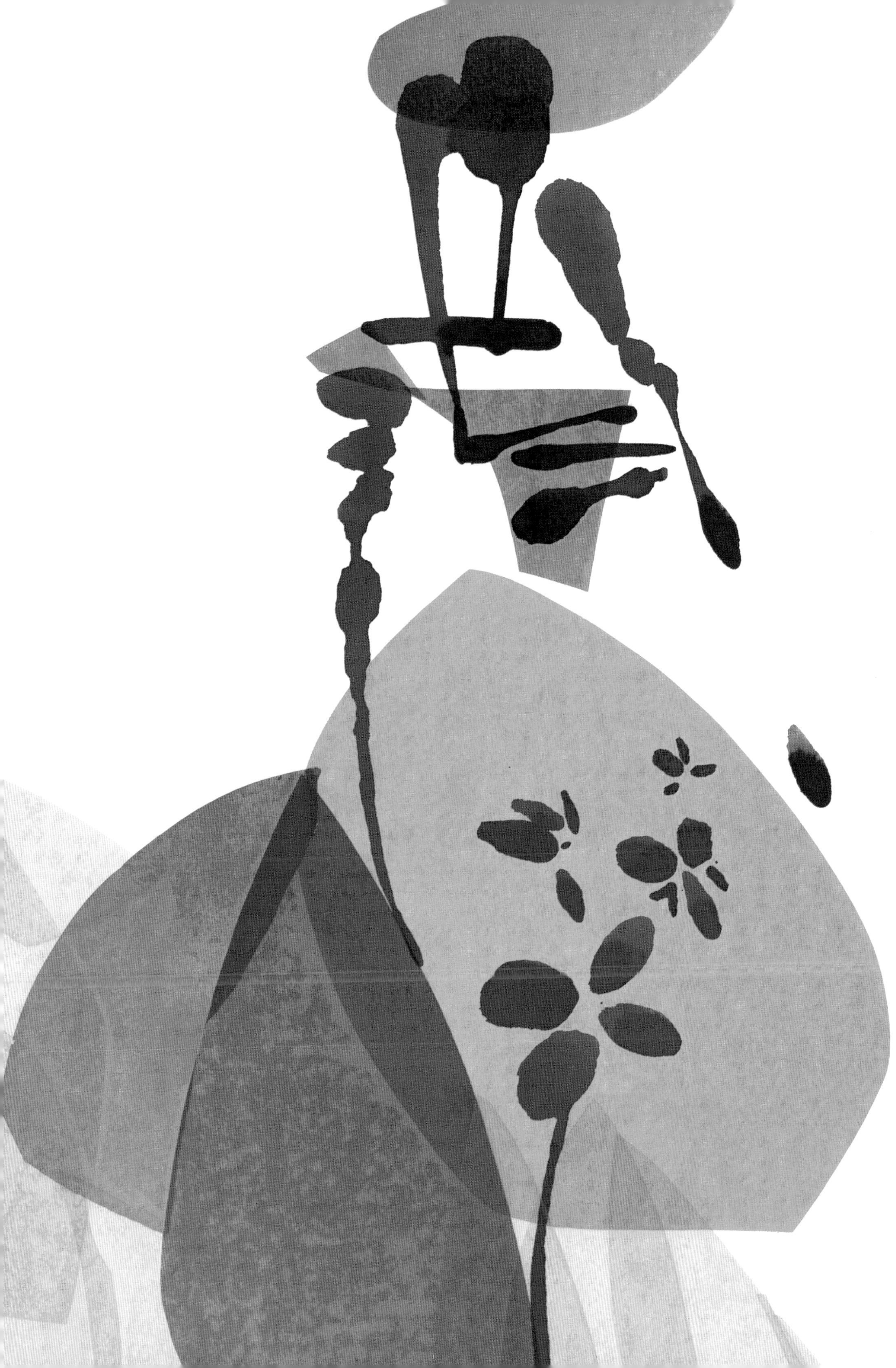

MATS
GUSTAFSON

Gustafson describes his work as 'an abstraction of fashion'. He aims to capture the idea of fashion through simplicity and abstraction, to propel the garment and the model beyond the specific moment. Gustafson approaches Illustration in a painterly way, working mainly with water-based media and pastel.

Yohji Yamamoto
Ink on paper
Commissioned by the designer, 1998

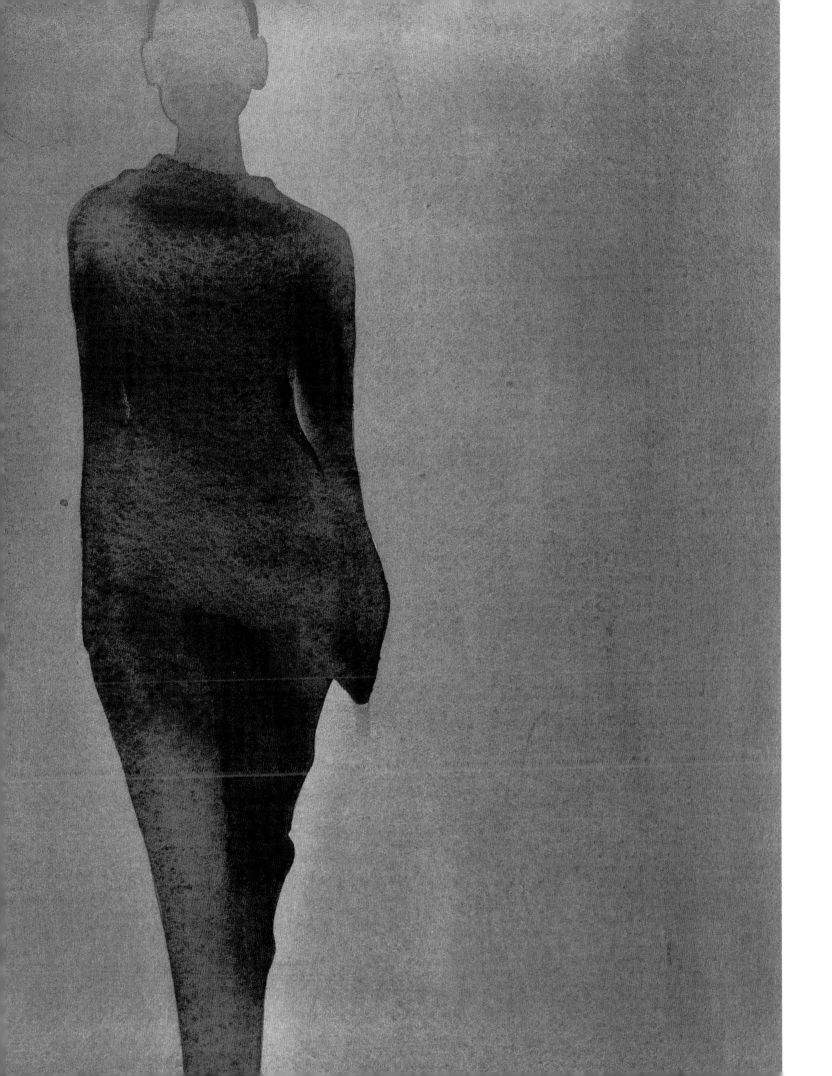

THIS PAGE
Watercolour and ink on paper
Artist's collection, 1999

OPPOSITE
Ink on paper
Stare Magazine, Spring 1999

KAREEM ILIYA

Iliya's work is usually described as being 'ethereal' and 'mystical'. He works with watercolour and ink on paper, often in vibrant colours through which figures and objects seem to burst and radiate.

THIS PAGE
Watercolour and ink on paper
Artist's collection, 1999

OPPOSITE
Watercolour and ink on paper
Bags: A Lexicon of Style, 1999

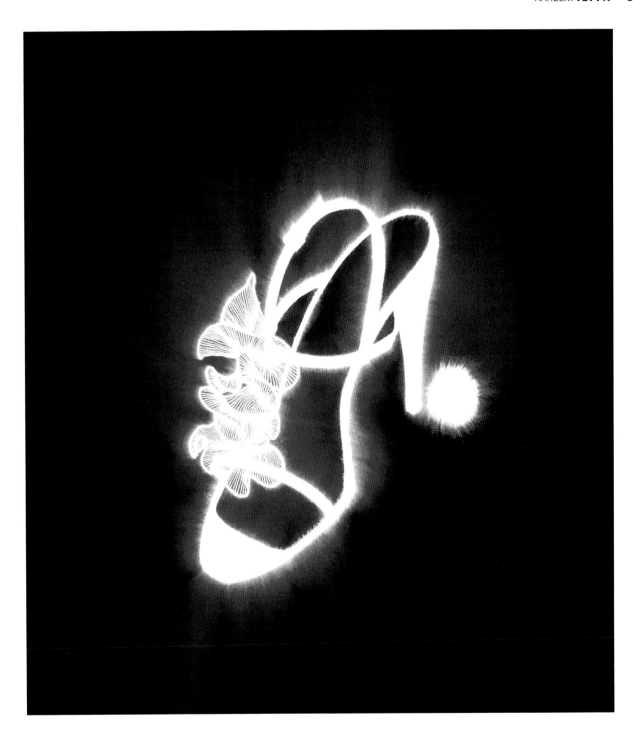

ABOVE
Bernard Figueroa shoe
Ink on paper
Invitation, 1999

OPPOSITE
Watercolour and ink on paper
Artist's collection, 1999

TANYA LING

Ling works quickly and impulsively with a medley of media. If her figures are meditative, her surfaces are raw and tactile. Ling says that her work is 'manic, emotional, full of feeling and impulsive'.

RIGHT
Mixed media on paper
Elle (USA) Fall/Winter Trend Report, 1999

OPPOSITE
Mixed media on paper
Artist's collection, 1999

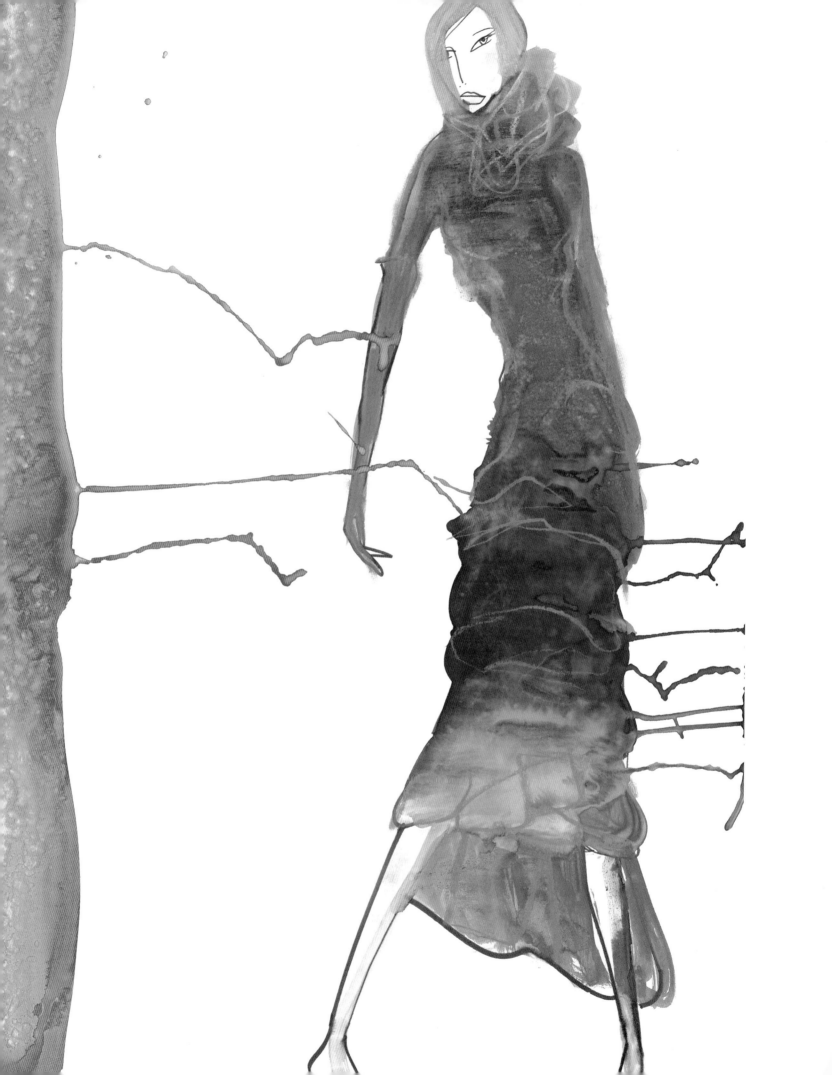

ABOVE
Prescriptives make-up on paper
Harper's Bazaar, September 1998

OPPOSITE
Yohji Yamamoto
Mixed media on paper
Joyce (Hong Kong), Summer 1999

RIGHT
Mixed media on paper
Elle (USA) Fall/Winter Trend Report, 1999

'I wanted to make my own collection, select all
the models and have them on the cover of a
fashion magazine'
Mixed media on paper
Artist's collection, 1999

Detail from 'I looked for the one my heart loves'
Mixed media on paper
Sotheby's New York Pulp Fashion catalogue, 1999

LORENZO MATTOTTI

Mattotti illustrates in a narrative fashion and he always tries to give personality to the women whom he draws. He starts with 'describing' the dress as much as possible and evoking an atmosphere. Mattotti's medium is oil pastels and he is inspired by paintings.

LORENZO MATTOTTI
RIGHT
Vivienne Westwood
Pastel and pencil on paper
The New Yorker, 1993

OPPOSITE
Fendi and Dolce & Gabbana
Pastel and pencil on paper
Playboy, 1997

PIET PARIS

Paris thinks of his illustrations as 'abstract fashion statements'. His colourful, graphic work is made with stencils created from an initial sketch and coloured with acrylic, gouache or pastel using a paint roller. Paris aims to achieve 'high fashion impact' with as few means as possible. He admires what is well and simply made, especially the paintings of Vermeer.

RIGHT
Kostas Murkudis
Mixed media on paper
De Telegraaf, October 1998

OPPOSITE
Mixed media on paper
Gasunie, 1998

ABOVE
Mixed media on paper
Gasunie, 1998

OPPOSITE
Mixed media on paper
Gasunie, 1998

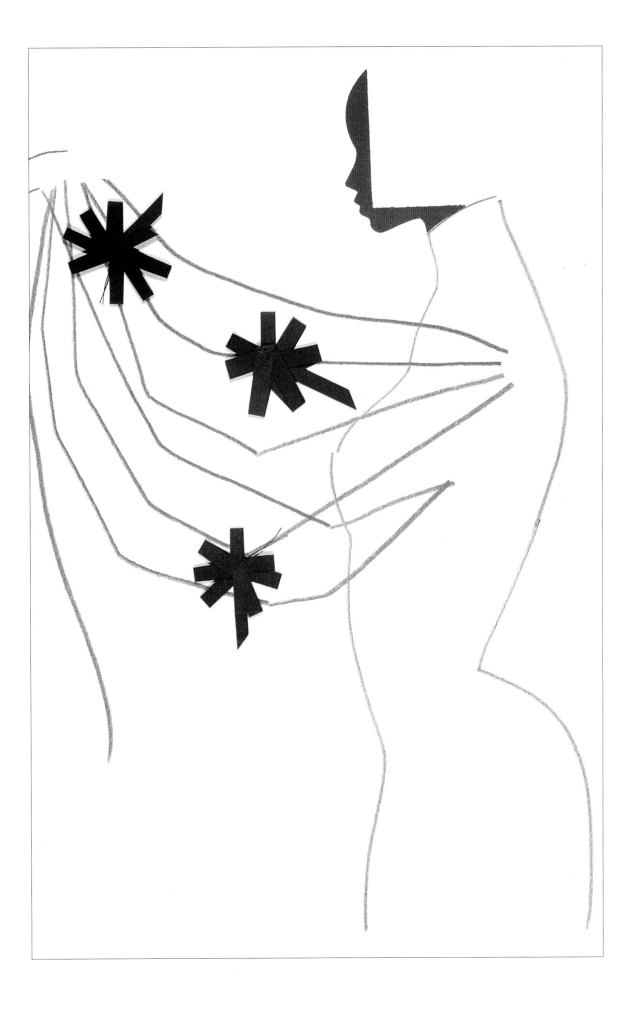

RIGHT
Mixed media on paper
Elle, 1999

OPPOSITE
Olivier Theyskens
De Telegraaf, October 1998

HIROSHI TANABE

Tanabe's drawings are often compared to traditional Japanese woodcuts. His ink drawings are mechanically transformed so that they sometimes seem to blur or move across the page. He explains: 'My drawings are so flat and simple that I try to give them a little more movement by putting things off-register.'

Alexander McQueen
Ink on paper
Blue Mode, 1998

ABOVE
Mixed media on paper
Anna Sui Cosmetics Catalogue, 1998

LEFT
Givenchy (by Alexander McQueen)
Ink on paper
Blue Mode, 1998

OPPOSITE
Marc Jacobs
Ink on paper
The New Yorker, 1995

RIGHT
Matsuda
Ink on paper
Matsuda catalogue, 1996

BELOW
Fendi baguette bags
Ink on paper
Bags: A Lexicon of Style, 1999

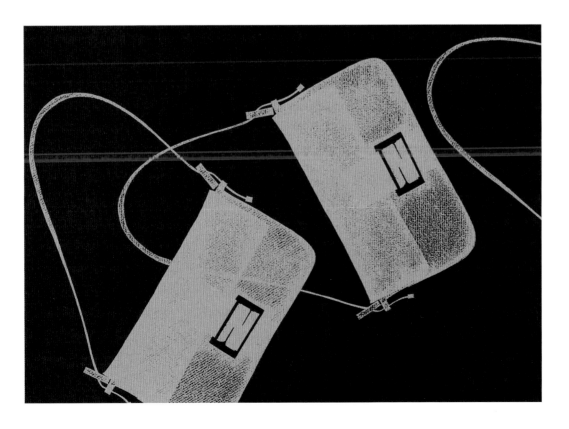

RUBEN TOLEDO

Working in a variety of media, Ruben Toledo aims to convey 'my sincere enthusiasm for our time, my wife and her work'. To Toledo, illustration is a personal and direct form of communication. 'While it is the most primitive of fashion presentations,' he says, 'it may be the most raw and human and lasting.'

OPPOSITE
Ink on paper
L'Uomo Vogue, 1999

THIS PAGE
Yohji Yamamoto
Ink on paper
L'Uomo Vogue, 1999

OVERLEAF
Various designers
Mixed media on paper
Interview, February 1999

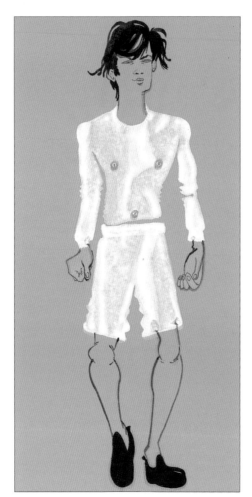
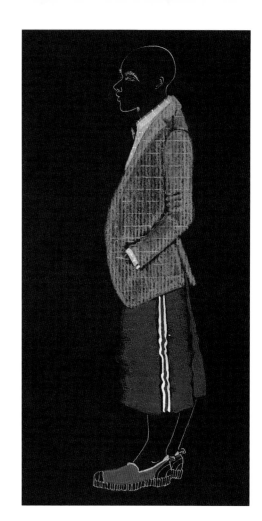

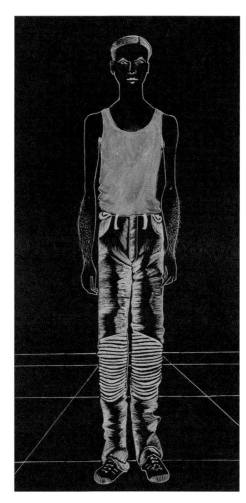
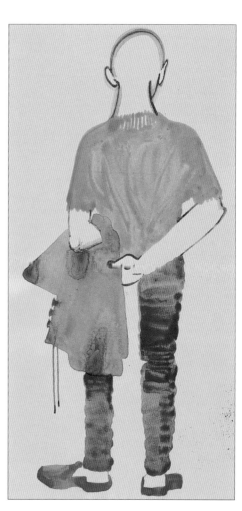

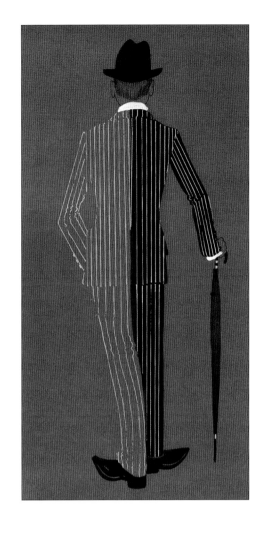
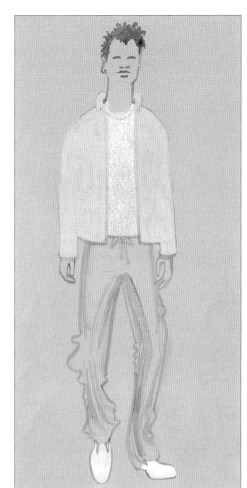

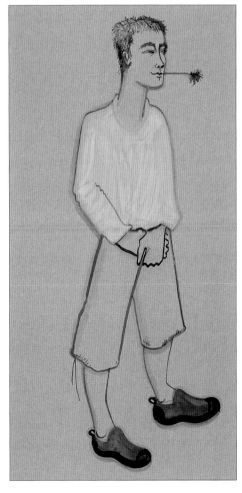
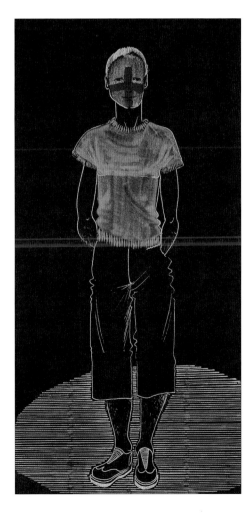

Prada

Paul Smith

LEFT TO RIGHT
Prada, Paul Smith, Donna Karan, Romeo Gigli
Ink on paper
L'Uomo Vogue, 1999

LISELOTTE WATKINS
Gucci & Giorgio Armani
Ink on paper
Artist's collection, 1999

ROBERT CLYDE **ANDERSON CARLOTTA** AMY **DAVIS** JEAN-PHILIPPE **DELHOMME**

JEFFREY **FULVIMARI KIRAZ** ANJA **KROENCKE** JORDI **LABANDA**

DEMETRIOS **PSILLOS** MAURICE **VELLEKOOP** LISELOTTE **WATKINS**

PART TWO
GAMINES&SOPHISTICATES

Whether they are drawing gamines or sophisticates, the artists in this section create imaginary worlds inhabited by vivid characters. They chronicle contemporary 'style tribes', borrowing elements of caricature and cartooning to do so, often with much humour and wit. They also reference, or reject, stereotypes of fashion representation, such as the static poses of the 1950s diva mannequins or Twiggy's doll-like slouch.

Carlotta, Amy Davis, Jeffrey Fulvimari, Kiraz and Liselotte Watkins draw big-eyed girls. Davis, however, deliberately draws 'ugly beauties' that break with stereotypical ideals of beauty, while Kiraz's girls are so representative of type that they have become known as 'Les Parisiennes'. Robert Clyde Anderson, Jean-Philippe Delhomme, Anja Kroencke, Jordi Labanda, Maurice Vellekoop and Demetrios Psillos create more haute-

monde characters. For example, Kroencke's abstract figures strike sophisticated mannequin poses, while Labanda's chic urbanites seem to 'live for the city'.

The illustrations in this section are figurative; this applies both to those who work abstractly and to those who work realistically. The illustrators are also highly accomplished artists, whether they draw with ink or markers, paint with gouache or create mixed media collages. The characters depicted in Gamines & Sophisticates are of all races and of different gender, reflecting the trend towards less gender-based lifestyle publications that serve the 'global village'. Although fantastic, these characters inhabit worlds that are available, at least to the fashionable – and to the sexy. Kiraz, Labanda, Psillos and Vellekoop often highlight sex appeal, once taboo, in their illustrations.

ROBERT CLYDE ANDERSON

Anderson's crisp, calligraphic illustrations – which he refers to as 'painted drawings' – are executed in pencil, transferred to acetate and then painted from the back, like animation cels. His work is highly figurative and is inspired by attractive, intelligent people who suggest that they have their own stories to tell.

SHOWTIMES
230 450 700 910

THIS PAGE
Michael Kors outfit
Acrylic on acetate
New York Magazine, 31 August 1998

OPPOSITE
Acrylic on acetate
The New York Times Magazine, March 1998

ABOVE AND RIGHT
Acrylic on acetate
Dayton's/Marshall Field's, Spring 1999

OPPOSITE
Acrylic on acetate
Artist's collection, 1998

CARLOTTA

Carlotta describes her wide-eyed, high-heeled Parisian girls as 'chic and funny', with an attitude that is at once 'ultra-feminine and militant'. Her sharp and precise drawings are executed with a black pen and coloured with gouache. Carlotta is inspired by Diana Vreeland's work for *Harper's Bazaar*.

ABOVE AND LEFT
Ink on paper
French *Lila*, 1998

OPPOSITE
Ink and gouache on paper
Artist's collection, 1999

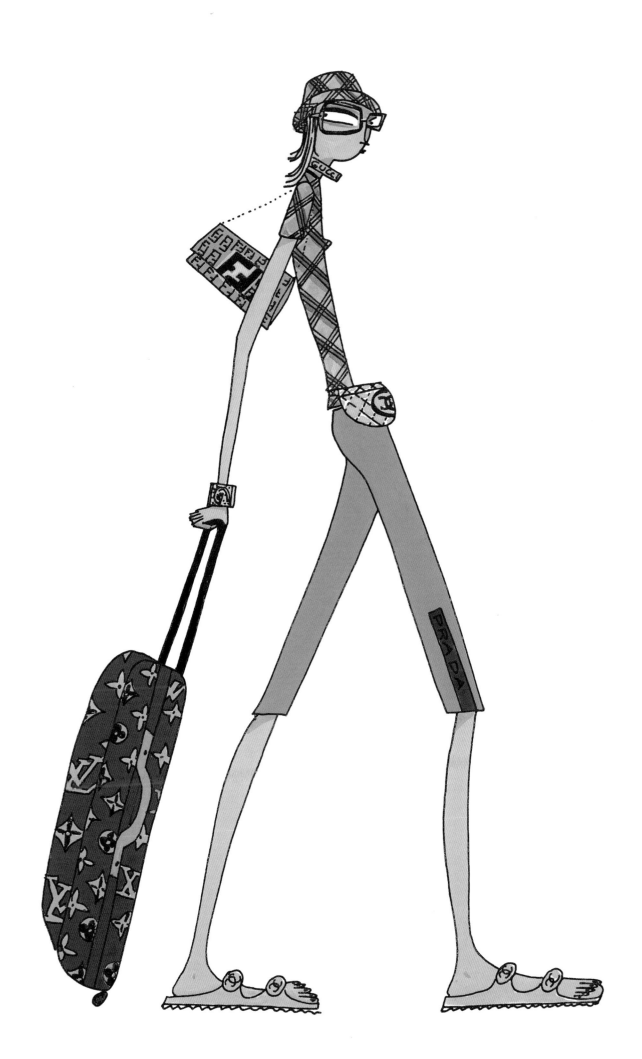

Chanel haute couture
Gouache and ink on paper
Artist's collection, 1999

ABOVE
Gouache and ink on paper
French *Elle*, 1997

OPPOSITE
Gouache and ink on paper
Vogue Hommes, 1996

AMY DAVIS

Davis challenges stereotypes of sophistication and beauty with her bodacious bad girls and 'ugly beauties', whom she describes as 'lo-fi and trashy'. Her drawings are executed in three steps. First, she makes an outline in pen and correction fluid (for texture). She then copies the outline onto clean paper and colours the sketch with coloured pencils and magic markers.

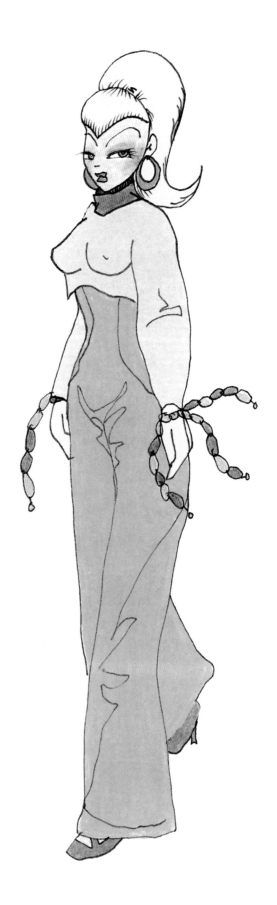

RIGHT
Thierry Mugler
Mixed media on paper
Paper, May 1996

OPPOSITE
'Chinese Noodles'
Left: shirt by Custo, skirt by Calvin Klein
Right: shirt by Pimpgear, pants by Starlette
Mixed media on paper
Paper, May 1999

THIS PAGE
Pucci
Mixed media on paper
Paper, February 1997

OPPOSITE
Yohji Yamamoto (left) and
Jean-Charles de Castelbajac (right)
Mixed media on paper
Paper, May 1996

JEAN-PHILIPPE DELHOMME

Painted with gouache on paper, Delhomme's softly coloured, fluid and tentative illustrations are infused with a spirit of 'optimistic irony' that transforms them into precise caricatures of the 'beautiful people'. Delhomme describes his work as 'documentary with a twist'.

Marie-Hélène de Taillac
Gouache on paper
Invitation, 1999

Raf Simons Men's Show, Paris
Gouache on paper
Artist's collection, 1998

YSL Men's Show, Paris
Gouache on paper
Artist's collection, 1998

ABOVE AND OPPOSITE
Marie-Hélène de Taillac
Gouache on paper
Promotions, Left Autumn 1998, Right Spring 1999

JEFFREY FULVIMARI

Fulvimari's serene characters, drawn in his signature blotchy line, are inspired by the women in his family. He says: 'I would like to think that my girls project a certain quality of kindness.' Fulvimari works two-dimensionally in pen and ink, and with a Macintosh computer.

Hussein Chalayan
Macintosh, Photoshop
Artist's collection, 1999

hussein chalayan fall 1999

ABOVE AND OPPOSITE
Ink on paper
Details from an installation at Global 33, New York, 1994

Macintosh, Photoshop
Tuka, Japan corporate calendar, 2000

KIRAZ

According to Kiraz, his Parisiennes are girls who are 'silly, but not wicked. They do a lot of window shopping and change boyfriends at the drop of a hat.' He is inspired by women, particularly Parisian women, 'who are always in a hurry, they take tiny steps'. He likes to pass time in cafés watching them go by. Kiraz paints with gouache on board.

RIGHT
Gouache on board
Nivea Cream promotion, May 1998

OPPOSITE
'Quand mon mari verra tout ce que j'ai acheté, il va hurler, me traiter de tous les noms. Alors je vais pleurer et bouder et finalement il me fera un beau cadeau pour se faire pardonner.'
Gouache on board
Gala, May 1998

KIRAZ

ABOVE

'J'ai eu tort de te prêter une robe, Chantal: il est
si ivre qu'il croit que c'est moi qui suis dedans!'
Gouache on board
Jours de France, March 1982

OPPOSITE

'Sauvons nous! J'ai entendu quelqu'un bailler!'
Gouache on board
Jours de France, November 1985

ANJA
KROENCKE

Kroencke's elegant figures subtly communicate their sophistication through pose and posture. Kroencke uses mixed media, including acrylic paint, gouache and collage, to create her simple and highly graphic illustrations. She describes her work as 'modern'.

Mixed media on paper
Madame Figaro, 1999

Mixed media on paper
New York City Opera mailer
Young Listeners Campaign, 1999

Mixed media on paper
New York City Opera poster
Young Listeners Campaign, 1999

ABOVE
'Lingerie', 1997
Mixed media on paper
Artist's collection

LEFT
Mixed media on paper
Madame, 1999

Mixed media on paper
Madame, 1999

JORDI
LABANDA

Labanda's sophisticated illustrations, peopled with elegant and intelligent figures, are painted in gouache and are imbued with a sense of humour. Labanda says that their strong, almost photographic, compositions express in him the fashion photographer 'that never came through'.

ABOVE
Alexander McQueen
Gouache on paper
AB, June 1998

OPPOSITE
Lawrence Steele
Gouache on paper
AB, June 1998

OPPOSITE
Lanvin
Gouache on paper
AB, 1999

BELOW
Oscar de la Renta
Gouache on paper
AB, 1999

Prada
Gouache on paper
AB, 1999

DEMETRIOS
PSILLOS

People with 'a certain air, a certain grace' inhabit the world that Psillos
illustrates, and caricatures. He describes these glamorous, haute-monde
creatures as 'sophisticated and surreal', adding: 'They are totally mad but they
just don't care.' Psillos paints with acrylic on paper or card and often incorporates
collage into his work.

THIS PAGE
'Girl Holding Antonio Berardi Bag'
Mixed media on paper
British *Vogue*, September 1997

OPPOSITE
'Girl with Lemon'
Mixed media on paper
British *Vogue*, August 1997

DEMETRIOS PSILLOS
LEFT
'Woman Wearing Missoni'
Mixed media on paper
Harper's Bazaar (USA), July 1999

OPPOSITE
'Pasha Pad'
Mixed media on paper
Wallpaper*, July/August 1998

MAURICE VELLEKOOP

Maurice Vellekoop approaches each drawing session as if it were a photo shoot in which he gets to be the stylist, make-up and hair people, and photographer. His illustrations are executed with felt pens and watercolours. Inspired by photography and by traditional cartooning styles, Vellekoop describes himself as 'a mild satirist'. The subjects of his satire are fashion and sex.

Dolce & Gabbana
Watercolour on paper
Wallpaper*, May/June 1997

THIS PAGE
DKNY, Alan Flusser

OPPOSITE
Kiton, Helmut Lang, Brooks Brothers
Watercolour on paper
Men's Fashions, The New York Times Magazine
22 March 1998

MAURICE VELLEKOOP
OPPOSITE
Missoni
Watercolour on paper
*Wallpaper**, May/June 1997

BELOW
Christian Dior Boutique, Valentino
Watercolour on paper
*Wallpaper**, November/December 1997

LISELOTTE
WATKINS

'Modern, simple and emotional' are the words Watkins uses to describe her work. Her illustrations and collages are made using Pantone papers and gouache. Watkins' contemporary girls are 'interesting and sympathetic, yet alluring and sexy'.

RIGHT
Mixed media
Amica, July 1999

OPPOSITE
Gucci
Mixed media
Amica, July 1999

ABOVE
Dolce & Gabbana
Mixed media
Amica, April 1999

LEFT
Cunni
Ink on paper
Artist's collection, 1999

RIGHT
Louis Vuitton
Mixed media
Amica, July 1999

ABOVE
Horoscopes
Mixed media
Amica, September 1999

RIGHT
Samsonite
Mixed media
Amica, July 1999

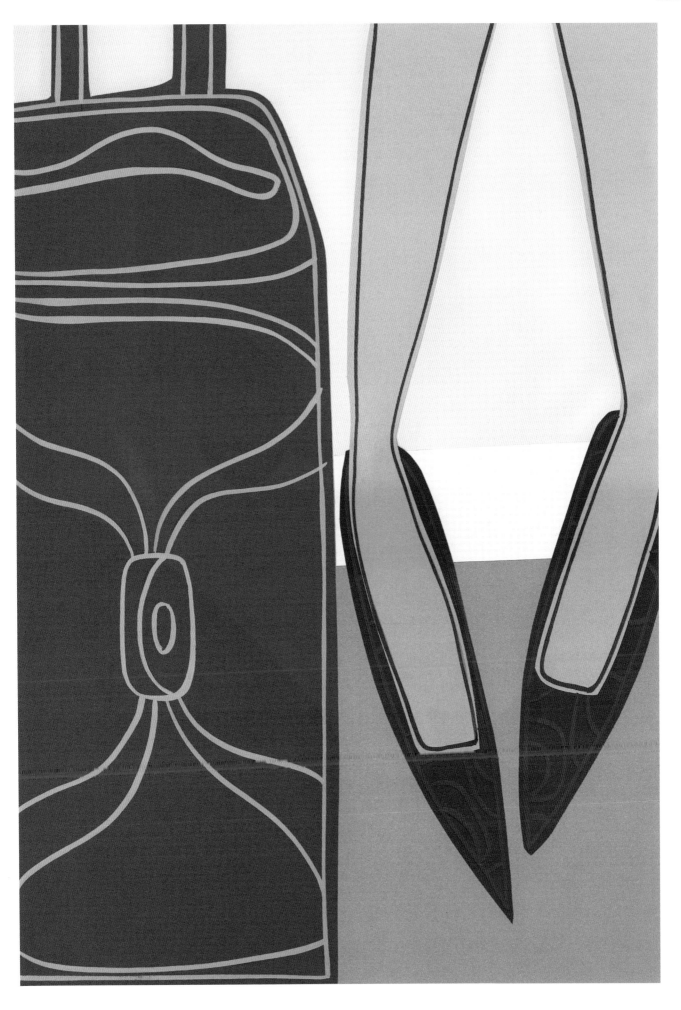

Ed. TSUWAKI
Comme des Garçons
Macintosh G3, Adobe Illustrator
Zola, February 1997

JASON **BROOKS** MICHAEL **ECONOMY** YOKO **IKENO** MAXINE **LAW** THIERRY **PEREZ**

GRAHAM **ROUNTHWAITE** KRISTIAN **RUSSELL** Ed. **TSUWAKI**

PART THREE
THE TECHNOCRATS

The computer is revolutionizing illustration. Each of the illustrators in the Technocrat section draw, but not as an end in itself. Technocrats are fascinated by the process of digitally transforming illustrations, and their handwork is the first step towards a final product that is computer-generated.

Of the Technocrats, Jason Brooks, Thierry Perez, Graham Rounthwaite and Ed. Tsuwaki are the most figurative, an approach that brings them closest to the Gamines & Sophisticates.

Brooks' glamorous, glossy characters exist in a candy-coloured boutique atmosphere, while Rounthwaite creates an urban environment peopled by cool, street-smart kids. Perez has transformed and enhanced his earlier, stridently sexy style of drawing in pastels with the computer.

Tsuwaki's characters are protean; his super-smooth, almost slick, elongated gamines border on the extraterrestrial.

The work of Michael Economy and Maxine Law is highly graphic, with heavy black outlines and flat layouts. Economy's style is an amalgam of Hanna Barbara, Japanimation and Pop, while Law's figures evoke 1960s poster art. Law's ads for Paul Smith were intended to have a retro, 'yellow submarine' feeling. In comparison, Yoko Ikeno's graphic work is more abstract, relying on silhouette and pose.

Kristian Russell's illustrations are best described as abstract and minimal. Russell relentlessly whittles and reduces his figures down to reflective surfaces. His eerie and artful characters seem to exist under glaring lights or through some trippy, psychedelic haze.

JASON BROOKS

Brooks' illustrations evoke 'a glossy parallel universe where everyone is beautiful'. His women are strong and confident ('not just girls in clothes'). They often look directly out of the page at the viewer.

LEFT
Macintosh G4, Adobe Photoshop
New York Interior, 1999

OPPOSITE
Prada
Macintosh G4, Adobe Photoshop
Elle (UK), November 1999

THIS PAGE
Alessandro Dell'Acqua
Macintosh G4, Adobe Photoshop
Elle (UK), November 1999

OPPOSITE
Girl in a Jacobsen Chair
Macintosh G4, Adobe Photoshop
Artist's collection, 1999

THIS PAGE
Macintosh G4, Adobe Photoshop
Artist's collection, 1999

OPPOSITE
Ink pen, Macintosh G4, Adobe Photoshop
German *Elle*, 1999

MICHAEL ECONOMY

In 1996 Economy abandoned his Sharpie markers and Chartpack coloured films in favour of a Macintosh computer. His 'vibrant and coy' illustrations are inspired by Pop Art and Japanamation. He describes his aesthetic as being that of a 'big-eye wee-wee teenage sex party!'.

ABOVE
Anna Sui
PowerMac 7200, Illustrator
Show invitation, Autumn 1997

RIGHT
Anna Sui Jeans/Gilmar
PowerMac 7200, Illustrator
Jeans mini poster, 1997

OPPOSITE
Anna Sui
PowerMac 7200, Illustrator
Logo, 1993

OVERLEAF
Celery Dollies
PowerMac 7200, Illustrator
Paper dolls for Anna Sui Jeans, 1997

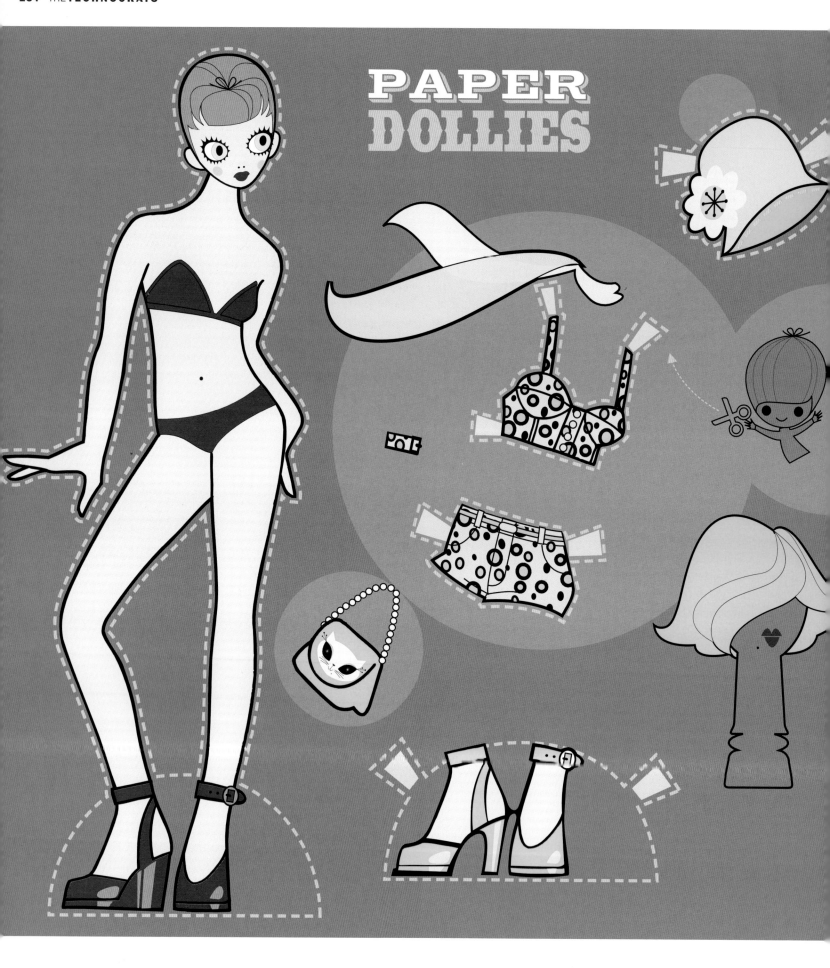

PAPER DOLLIES

MICHAEL ECONOMY

THIS PAGE
Graffiti Kids
PowerMac 7200, Illustrator
Sweater Magazine, 1998

OPPOSITE
Scorpio Gal
PowerMac 7200, Illustrator
B Magazine, 1997

YOKO IKENO

Inspired by her everyday life, Ikeno aims to 'express subtle feeling and attitude with minimum lines and surprising colour'. Her abstract figurative illustrations are drawn with pencil and watercolour and transformed on the Macintosh.

OPPOSITE
Lanvin
Macintosh G3, Adobe Photoshop
Artist's collection, 1999

BELOW
Macintosh G3, Adobe Photoshop
Artist's collection, 1999

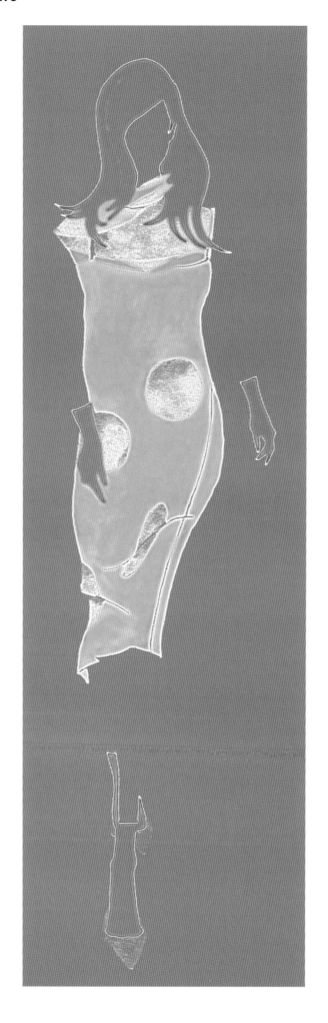
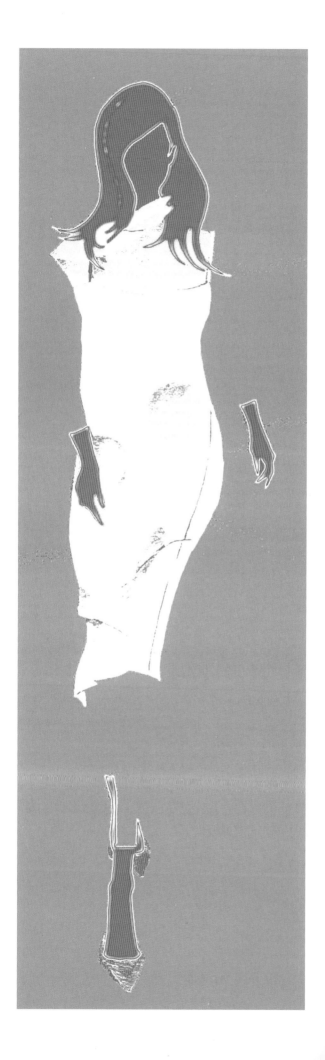

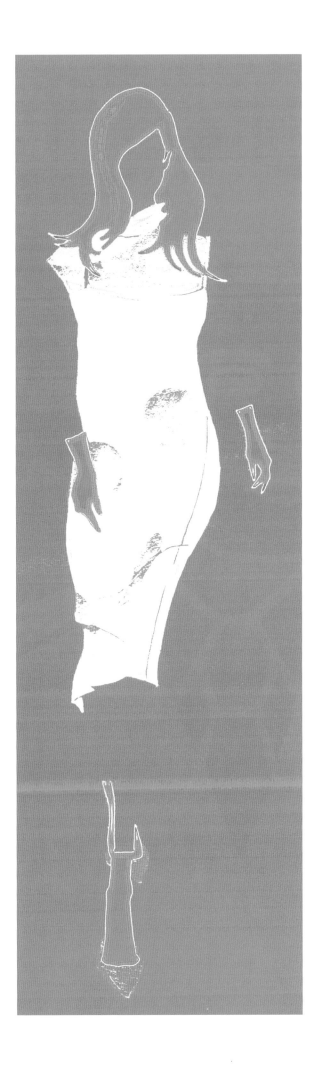

ABOVE
Macintosh G3, Adobe Photoshop
Artist's collection, 1999

LEFT
Martine Sitbon
Macintosh G3, Adobe Photoshop
Artist's collection, 1999

MAXINE LAW

Law describes her work as 'strong, bold, quite quirky and slightly cartoonish'. She is inspired by David Hockney's draughtsmanship and by the way that Henri Matisse and Howard Hodgkin use colour.

OPPOSITE
Macintosh G3, Illustrator
Esquire (UK), November 1997

BELOW AND RIGHT
Paul Smith
Macintosh G3, Illustrator
Advertising campaign, Autumn/Winter 1996
Courtesy of Paul Smith Ltd.

OVERLEAF
Paul Smith
Macintosh G3, Illustrator
Advertising campaign, Spring/Summer 1997
Courtesy of Paul Smith Ltd.

THIERRY
PEREZ

Thierry Perez discovered the computer in 1999. In order to 'keep emotion' in his work he always starts with a hand drawing, black lines on paper, before transferring it to the computer. Perez is no minimalist. Asked to describe his work, he says: 'I've always loved sensuality and eroticism as well as very extreme characters. I also love to turn weird things into the poetic and the surrealistic.'

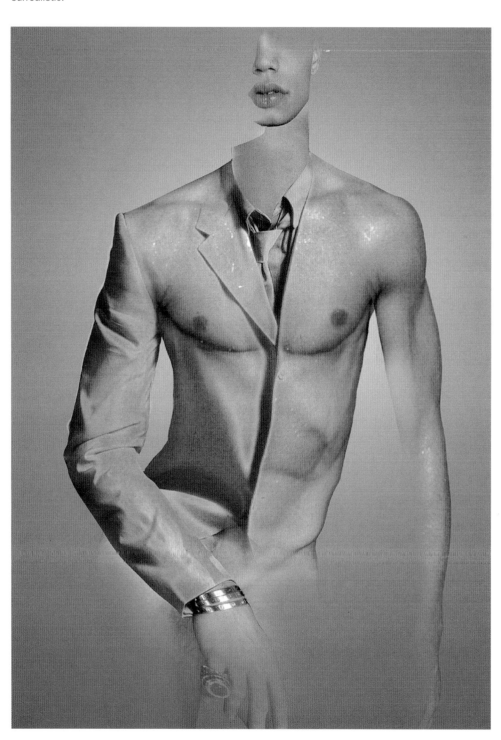

RIGHT
Macintosh G3, Photoshop
Artist's collection, 1999

OPPOSITE
Pascal Humbert
Macintosh G3, Photoshop
Artist's collection, 1999

OVERLEAF
Macintosh G3, Photoshop
Artist's collection, 1999

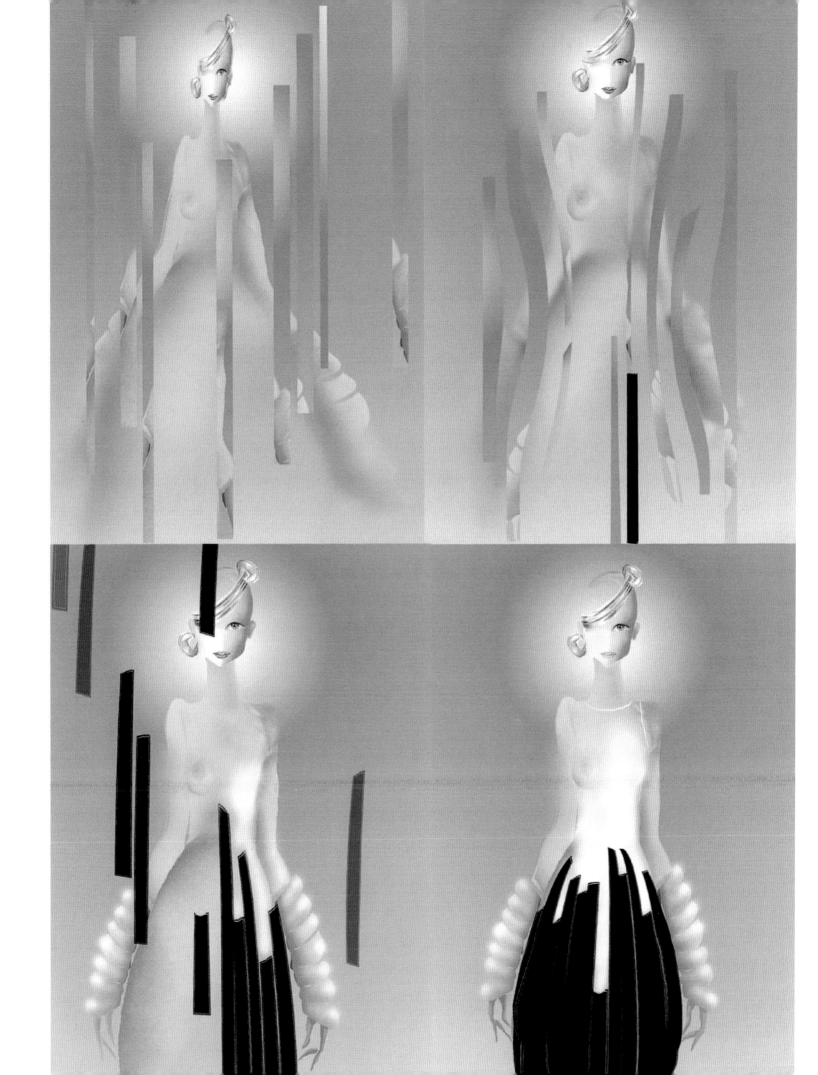

T.PEREZ

GRAHAM ROUNTHWAITE

Rounthwaite is inspired by 'real people', rather than fashion. His cool kids are unselfconscious and they brighten the muted urban environments that they inhabit. Rounthwaite says that all he ever wanted was his drawings 'to mean something to the regular young person in the street and reflect their aspirations'.

OPPOSITE AND BELOW
Macintosh G3, Photoshop
silverTab® Advertising campaign, 1999

Macintosh G3, Photoshop
silverTab® Advertising campaign, 1998

Macintosh G3, Photoshop
silverTab® Advertising campaign, 1998

KRISTIAN RUSSELL

Russell's extreme, electric work is hard-edged. Using Illustrator, Russell puts his initial sketches 'through their paces', distilling them into abstractions of form and reflective surface. He says that his work has a 'split personality' that others have described as 'Art Nouveau meets Hype Williams' and 'Aubrey Beardsley meets the Matrix'. Russell is inspired by many things, but music has a major influence on his work.

LEFT
White jumpsuit
Macintosh G3, Illustrator
Scene Magazine, June 1998

OPPOSITE
Maharishi by Maharishi, Marina Kereklidou & Burfitt
Macintosh G3, Illustrator
Artist's collection, 1998

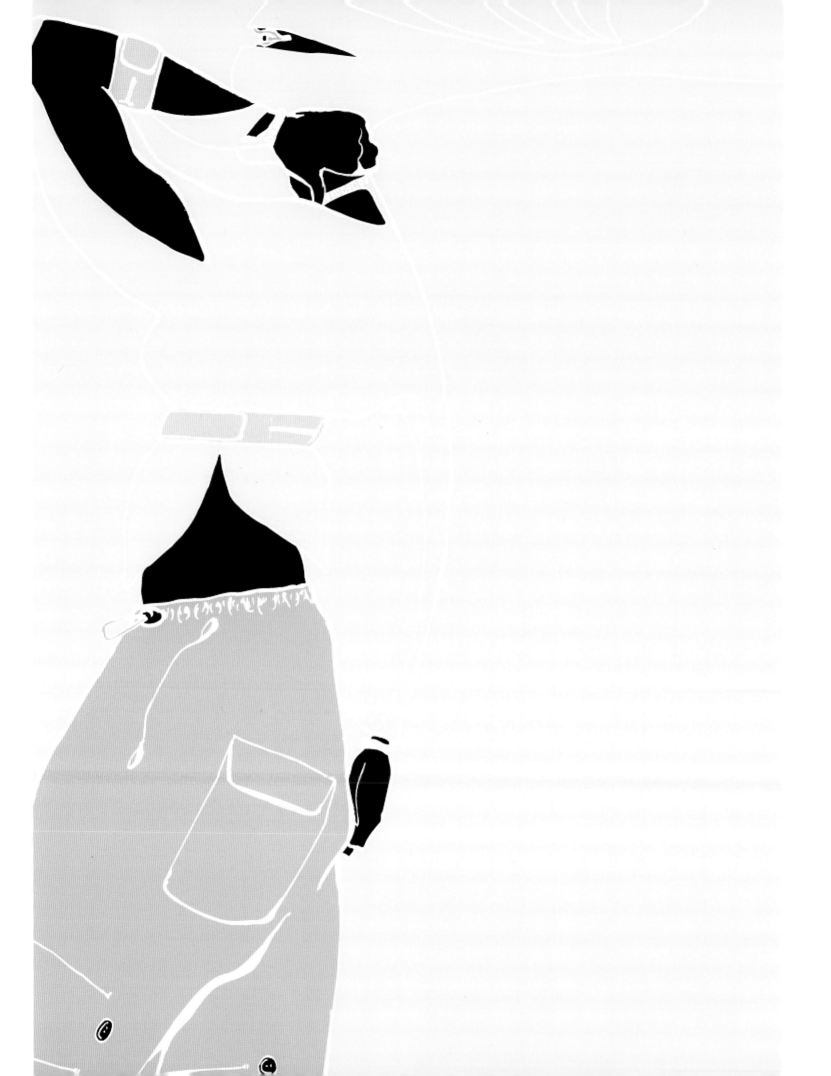

OPPOSITE
As Four
Macintosh G3, Illustrator
Nylon Magazine, March 1999

LEFT
Shark coat by Vexed Generation
Macintosh G3, Illustrator
Made for Vexed Generation, September 1998

BELOW
Bala dress by Vexed Generation
Macintosh G3, Illustrator
Made for Vexed Generation, September 1998

ABOVE
The Girls
Macintosh G3, Illustrator
Commissioned by *Frank Magazine*, April 1998

OPPOSITE
Helen Tibbling
Macintosh G3, Illustrator
Produced for a fashion show, May 1999

Ed. TSUWAKI

Tsuwaki developed his current style in 1994 when he started using the computer for illustration. His smooth, elongated figures are wide-eyed and knowing, with the touch of the extraterrestrial about them. Illustrating, says Tsuwaki, is 'like giving birth to the other self in me'.

OPPOSITE
'The Girls from Dublin'
Macintosh G3, Adobe Illustrator
In Natural, October 1996

THIS PAGE
'Kate the Cowgirl'
Macintosh G3, Adobe Illustrator
Artist's collection, December 1998

OVERLEAF
'White'
Macintosh G3, Adobe Illustrator
Vogue Nippon, pre-launch issue, September 1998

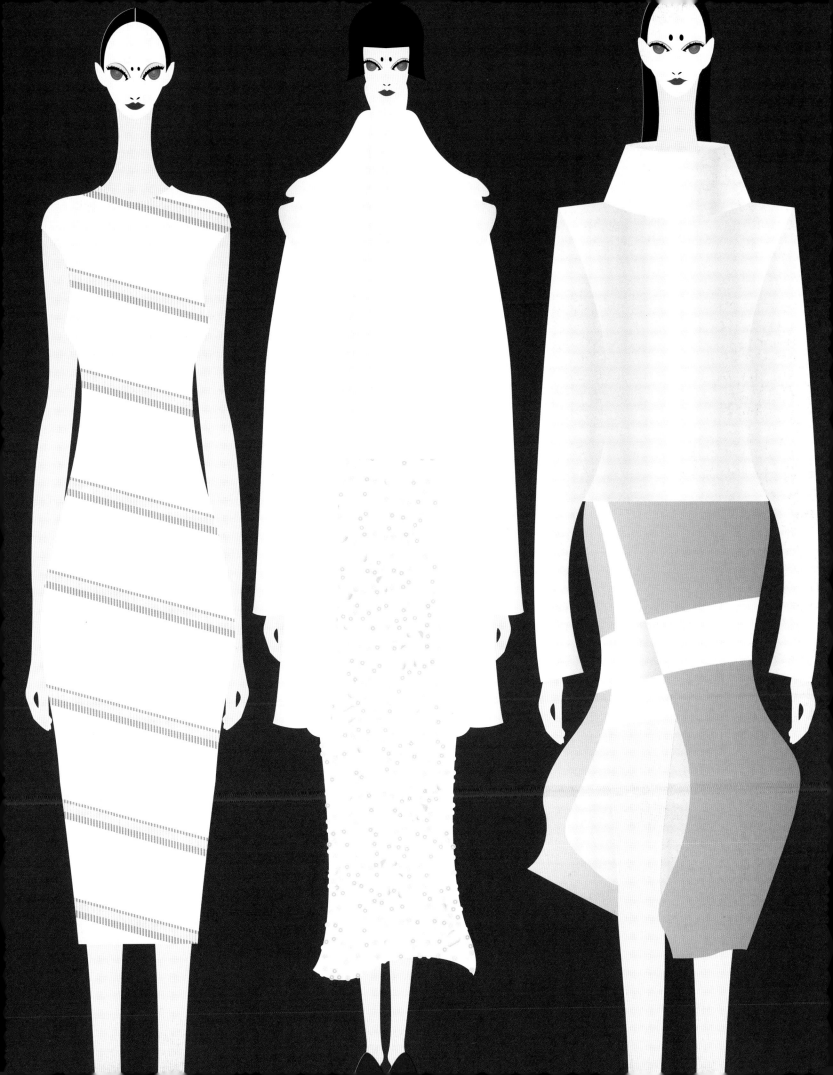

NIETZSCHE

Albert Camu

JEAN-PAUL SARTRE

Ed. TSUWAKI

ABOVE

'Funny Face', Ralph Lauren Collection
Macintosh G3, Adobe Illustrator
Vogue Nippon, September 1999

RIGHT

'Funny Face', Narcisco Rodriguez
Macintosh G3, Adobe Illustrator
Vogue Nippon, September 1999

BIOGRAPHIES

RUBEN ALTERIO

ROBERT CLYDE ANDERSON

FRANÇOIS BERTHOUD

Ruben Alterio was born in 1949 in Argentina into a family of artists. He studied at L'Ecole des Beaux-Arts in Buenos Aires before settling in Paris. Alterio's work has been exhibited in numerous galleries and museums. He has illustrated books for Editions Assouline, Editions Aubier and Editions du Seuil. In 1999 Alterio entered into a theatrical collaboration, *Peines de cœur d'une chatte française*, with director Alfredo Arias. His illustrations for this work were published as a book.

Alterio has worked with major advertising agencies and magazines since the 1980s. His editorial work has appeared in many publications, including *Elle, Madame Figaro, Frankfurter Allgemeine Magazin, Deutsche Vogue, Marie Claire, Mirabella, New York Magazine* and *The New Yorker*. Among Alterio's corporate clients are Boucheron, Celine, Chanel, Crédit Lyonnais, DIM, Ermenegildo Zegna, Escada, Galeries Lafayette, Kenzo, L'Oréal, Lancôme, Piaget, Taittinger and Neiman Marcus, for whom he illustrated a 36-page insert in 1997.

CONTACT:
**2ᵉ Bureau, 13 rue d'Aboukir, 75002 Paris
T: (33) (0)(1) 42 33 93 18
F: (33) (0)(1) 40 26 41 53
e-mail: sylvie.flaure@wanadoo.fr**

Robert Clyde Anderson grew up on a farm in Louisiana. He started drawing at the age of two. Later, he studied fine art and design at Louisiana State University. After graduating with a BFA, Anderson continued to study figure drawing and painting on his own. He worked for ten years in advertising in New Orleans before moving to New York in 1989, where he began working as a freelance illustrator. Anderson lives in New York City.

Anderson counts *Details, Fortune, House & Garden, Mademoiselle, New York Magazine, The New York Times Magazine, Travel & Leisure, Vogue* and *Wallpaper** among his editorial clients. His corporate clients include AT&T, Barneys New York, Bergdorf Goodman, Dayton's, ESPN, Estée Lauder, The Gap, IBM, J. Crew, Kenneth Cole, Le Printemps, Lincoln Center, Marshall Field's, Microsoft, Moet & Chandon, Neiman Marcus and Turner Broadcasting. Additionally, Anderson has illustrated and lettered book jackets for Chronicle Books, Doubleday, Farrar, Straus & Giroux and St Martin's Press, among others.

CONTACT (USA):
**Art Department, 48 Greene Street, New York, NY 10013
T: (1) (212) 925 4222
F: (1) (212) 925 4422
e-mail: artdept@panix.com**

CONTACT (UK):
**Art Department, 113 Canalot Studios, 222 Kensal Road, London W10 5BN
T: (44) (020) 8968 8881
F: (44) (020) 8968 8801
e-mail: lucy@artdept-london.co.uk
website: www.art-dept.com**

François Berthoud was born in Switzerland in 1961. He studied graphic design and illustration in Lausanne and graduated in 1982. He then moved to Milan to work for Condé Nast. His first published works were comics and illustrations for avant-garde magazines. During the 1980s he was one of the principal contributors to *Vanity*, illustrating fashion stories and covers. Exhibition catalogues of his work have been published by Bartsch & Chariau. His studio is in Milan.

Berthoud's work has appeared in *Amica, Harper's Bazaar, Interview, L'Uomo Vogue, Marie Claire, The New York Times Magazine, The New Yorker, Visionaire*, as well as Italian, French, German, Spanish and British editions of *Vogue*. Among his corporate clients are Alessi, Galeries Lafayette, The Gap, Hermès, Jil Sander, Krizia, Malo, Prada, Romeo Gigli, and The Ginza, Japan.

CONTACT (FRANCE):
**Yannick Morisot, 10, cité d'Angoulême, 75001 Paris
T: 33 (0)(1) 43 38 02 01
F: 33 (0)(1) 43 38 54 08
e-mail: kyannick@aol.com**

CONTACT (USA):
**Morisot Inc, 225 Lafayette Street, New York, NY 10012
T: (1) (212) 625 1225
F: (1) (212) 625 1845**

OPPOSITE
DEMETRIOS PSILLOS
'Girl wearing breast cancer tee shirt'
Mixed media on paper
British *Vogue*, June 1999

JASON BROOKS

Jason Brooks was born in London in 1969. He studied graphic design and illustration at St Martins and graduated with an honours degree. In 1991 Brooks received the British *Vogue*/Sotheby's Cecil Beaton Award for illustration. He later completed a Masters in illustration from The Royal College of Art. Brooks lives and works in London.

Brooks's work has appeared in *Detour, Elle, In Style, The Face, Harper's Bazaar, Visionaire* and British and French editions of *Vogue*, among other publications. His corporate clients include British Airways, Fabergé, Finlandia, L'Oréal, Ogilvy & Mather and Mercedes Benz.

CONTACT (USA):
UNIT NYC, 125 Cedar Street, 2N, New York, NY 10006
T: (1) (212) 766 4117
F: (1) (212) 766 4227

CONTACT (EUROPE):
UNIT CMA
Egelantiersstraat 143
1015 ra Amsterdam
T: (31) (0)(20) 530 6000
F: (31) (0)(20) 530 6001
website: www.unit_amsterdam.com

CARLOTTA

Carlotta was born in Lyons, France. She studied fashion design at L'Ecole des Beaux-Arts and at Studio Berçot in Paris, where she is now a professor. A book of her work, *Carlotta A to Z*, was published by Japanese Gap in 2000. Carlotta lives in Paris with her husband and son.

Carlotta's illustrations have appeared in many publications, including *Elle, Elle International, Mademoiselle, Manhattan File, Mirabella, The New Yorker, Spur Japan, Traveler, Visionaire, Vogue* and *Vogue Hommes*. In addition, she has covered fashion for *Libération*. Among her corporate clients are DIM, Galeries Lafayette, L'Oréal, Monoprix, Perrier Jouet, Le Printemps, Trois Suisse and La Ville de Paris.

CONTACT (FRANCE):
Carole Glass, 1, rue du Louvre, 75001 Paris
T: (33) (0)(1) 42 61 50 11
F: (33) (0)(1) 40 15 02 38

CONTACT (USA):
Kramer + Kramer, 156 Fifth Avenue, New York, NY 10010
T: (1) (212) 645 8787
F: (1) (212) 645 9591

CONTACT (JAPAN):
Fumie Shimoji, Jeu de Paume, Tokyo
T: (81) (0)(3) 3486 0532
F: (81) (0)(3) 3486 0534

AMY DAVIS

Amy Davis was born on Long Island, New York in 1968. She received a degree in illustration from the Rhode Island School of Design in 1990. Davis has participated in many group exhibitions, including a show at the Holly Solomon Gallery in New York City in 1999. Her work was included in *From AbFab to Zen* (D.A.P., 1999). Davis lives in San Francisco, where she works as a freelance illustrator and plays in a rock band with her husband.

Davis's work has appeared in American and Japanese publications, including *Composite, Giant Robot, Hanatsubaki, Seventeen* and *Teen People*. She illustrates the monthly 'Style Fiends' column for *Paper* magazine and illustrated the May 1997 cover. Davis has done work for Beams and for Nine West and she also has designed for a clothing line called Cosmic Girls.

CONTACT:
T+F: (1) (415) 386 0731

JEAN-PHILIPPE DELHOMME

Jean-Philippe Delhomme was born in 1959 in Nanterre, France. He graduated from L'Ecole Nationale des Arts Décoratifs in 1985 with a degree in animation. Delhomme began working as an illustrator in 1983. His work has been exhibited internationally, including a show at James Danzinger Gallery in New York in 1994. A book of his work, *Polaroids de Jeunes Filles*, was published by Albin Michel in 1990 and by Korinsha in 1994. Delhomme has designed film posters for Pedro Almodovar's *Tie Me Up! Tie Me Down!* and Kenneth Branagh's movie, *Peter's Friends*.

Delhomme's work has appeared in French *Glamour, House & Garden, The New Yorker, Town & Country*, as well as in British, French and Japanese editions of *Vogue*. His corporate clients include Barneys New York, for whom he produced a groundbreaking series of advertisements between 1993 and 1996, and Saab, for whom he directs animation films.

CONTACT:
Philippe Arnaud, 3, rue Valadon, 75007 Paris
T: (33) (0)(1) 45 56 00 33
F: (33) (0)(1) 45 56 01 33
e-mail: apa@clubinternet.fr

MICHAEL ECONOMY

Michael Economy was born in the Blue Ridge mountains of Virginia in 1960. He began drawing before he started school and later was awarded a scholarship to study graphic design and fashion illustration in Atlanta. He moved to New York in 1981 and started working as a freelance illustrator. Economy made his first trip to Japan in 1986 and returned to live there for a year in 1988. His work was exhibited at Parco Gallery, Japan in 1999 with Katsura Moshino. In 1999 Korinsha published a book of Economy's work, *I Love ME*. He is the Creative Director of Fine Clothing for young women.

Economy's work has appeared editorially in *Mademoiselle, Paper, Seventeen, Visionaire* and *Vogue*. His corporate clients include Anna Sui, Bloomingdale's, Deee-Lite, Elektra, MTV, Nick at Nite, Screaming Mimi's, Todd Oldham and Wigstock, among others.

CONTACT:
526 West 26th Street, Suite 1020, New York, NY 10001
T: (1) (212) 337 9760
F: (1) (212) 337 9628

JEFFREY FULVIMARI

Jeffrey Fulvimari was born in Akron, Ohio. He received a BFA from the Cooper Union, New York. In 1993 Fulvimari was given commissions by *Interview* and Barneys New York, launching his career as an illustrator. Since then his work has been exhibited in Japan at Parco Gallery in 1998 with Hiroshi Tanabe and in 1999 at CWC Gallery with Keiji Ito. Fulvimari designed a line of mannequins for Pucci in 1996 and in 1999 launched 'Teary' mints with Mikakuto. A book of his work, *It's O.K. and Everything's Gonna Be Alright*, was published by Korinsha in 1998. Fulvimari illustrated the boxed set, 'Ella Fitzgerald: The Complete Songbooks' (Verve), which won a Grammy award in 1985 for best CD package.

Fulvimari's work has appeared in *Allure, C22 Magazine, Figaro* (Japan), *Glamour, Harper's Bazaar, Interview, Mademoiselle, The New York Times Magazine, Seventeen, Travel & Leisure* and *Visionaire*, as well as British editions of *Elle* and *Marie Claire* and American and Spanish editions of *Vogue*. His corporate clients include Asia Beat, Helmut Lang, Anna Sui, Mikakuto, MTV, Neiman Marcus, Gyuotto by Senshu-kai, Sony Music Entertainment, Tu-ka Phone, Hush Puppies, Parco, Afterthoughts and The Museum of Modern Art.

CONTACT (USA):
CWC International, 462 Broadway, Suite 500, New York, NY 10013
T: (1) (212) 966 9093
F: (1) (212) 966 9076
e-mail: agent@cwc-i.com

CONTACT (JAPAN):
Cross World Connections (CWC), 1-6, 3F, Daikanyama-cho, Shibuya-ku, Tokyo
T: (81) (0)(3) 3496 0745
F: (81) (0)(3) 3496 0747
e-mail: agent@cwctokyo.com
website: www.cwctokyo.com

TOBIE GIDDIO

Tobie Giddio was born in 1963 on the New Jersey shore. She graduated from the Fashion Institute of Technology in 1986 with a BFA in Illustration and later taught in the illustration department there. An exhibition of her work was held in Japan at CWC Gallery in 2000. Giddio currently lives in New York City where she studies West African dance and practises yoga.

Giddio's work has appeared in *George, Glamour, Harper's Bazaar, Interview, Manhattan File, Marie Claire, Mode, The New York Times Magazine, The New Yorker, United Airlines Hemispheres* and American and Japanese editions of *Vogue*. She also illustrated several trend reports for *Harper's Bazaar*. Her corporate clients include Ann Taylor, Bergdorf Goodman, Garnet Hill, Giorgio Armani, Philip Morris, Pucci Mannequins, Revlon and Tocca.

CONTACT (USA):
**CWC International, 462 Broadway, Suite 500, New York NY 10013
T: (1) (212) 966 9093
F: (1) (212) 966 9076
e-mail: agent@cwc-i.com**

CONTACT (JAPAN):
**Cross World Connections (CWC) 1-6, 3F, Daikanyama-cho, Shibuya-ku, Tokyo
T: (81) (0)(3) 3496 0745
F: (81) (0)(3) 3496 0747
e-mail: agent@cwctokyo.com
website: www.cwctokyo.com**

MATS GUSTAFSON

Mats Gustafson was born in 1951 in Sweden. He studied at the National College of Fine Arts in Stockholm and graduated from the Scandinavian Drama Institute with a degree in costume and stage design. He began his career as an illustrator in Sweden even before graduation. His first international commission was from British *Vogue* in 1978, followed by American *Vogue* and *Andy Warhol's Interview*. In 1980 Gustafson moved to New York where he lives and works today. Gustafson's work has been internationally exhibited. Limited edition catalogues of his work have been published by Galerie Bartsch & Chariau, Munich, in 1993 and 1998.

Gustafson's work has appeared in many publications including *Harper's Bazaar, The New York Times Magazine, The New Yorker, Visionaire,* French and Japanese editions of *Vogue* and *Vogue Italia,* with whom he has a longstanding collaboration. His corporate client list includes Bergdorf Goodman, Galeries Lafayette, Nike and Shiseido, among others. Gustafson has also collaborated with Comme des Garçons, Romeo Gigli and Yohji Yamamoto.

CONTACT:
**Art & Commerce, 755 Washington Street, New York, NY 10014
T: (1) (212) 206 0737
F: (1) (212) 463 7267
e-mail: www.artandcommerce.com**

YOKO IKENO

Yoko Ikeno was born in Kanagawa, Japan in 1969 and studied at the Tokyo University of Foreign Language. She left Japan in 1991 to live between Europe and the USA. Ikeno started to do figurative illustrations while living in Milan and working for a fashion designer. She later began working as a freelance illustrator in Paris. Ikeno settled in Brooklyn, New York in 1998, where she lives with her husband and cat. Her work was exhibited at Gen Art in New York in 1999.

Ikeno's illustrations have appeared in *Nylon Magazine.* Among her corporate clients are Denver International Airport, Harvey Nichols, Max & Co., MTV and Swissair.

CONTACT (USA):
**Art Department, 48 Greene Street, New York, NY 10013
T: (1) (212) 925 4222
F: (1) (212) 925 4422
e-mail: artdept@panix.com**

CONTACT (UK):
**Art Department, 113 Canalot Studios, 222 Kensal Road, London W10 5BN
T: (44) (020) 8968 8881
F: (44) (020) 8968 8801
e-mail: lucy@artdept-london.co.uk
website: www.art-dept.com**

KAREEM ILIYA

Kareem Iliya was born in Beirut, Lebanon in 1967. He grew up in Texas and studied textiles and clothing at The University of Texas at Austin. After graduation he continued his studies at the Fashion Institute of Technology in New York. While working as a designer, Iliya began freelancing as an illustrator. One of his first commissions was a drawing for the Christmas window of Spazio Romeo Gigli in New York. Iliya is based in New York City.

Iliya's illustrations have appeared in *Interview*, *The New Yorker*, *W*, *Visionaire* and the Japanese and Korean editions of *Vogue*, among other publications. His corporate clients include Cerruti, Barneys New York, Bergdorf Goodman, Neiman Marcus, Rugiada Japan and Shiseido. His work was featured in *Shoes: A Lexicon of Style* (Rizzoli, 1999) and he illustrated the cover of *Handbags: A Lexicon of Style* (Rizzoli, 2000) (UK title, *Bags*, 1999)

CONTACT (USA):
Art Department, 48 Greene Street, New York, NY 10013
T: (1) (212) 925 4222
F: (1) (212) 925 4422
e-mail: artdept@panix.com

CONTACT (UK):
Art Department, 113 Canalot Studios, 222 Kensal Road, London W10 5BN
T: (44) (020) 8968 8881
F: (44) (020) 8968 8801
e-mail: lucy@artdept-london.co.uk
website: www.art-dept.com

CONTACT (JAPAN):
Cross World Connections (CWC), 1-6, 3F, Daikanyama-cho, Shibuya-ku, Tokyo
T: (81) (0)(3) 3496 0745
F: (81) (0)(3) 3496 0747
e-mail: agents@cwctokyo.com
website: www.cwctokyo.com

KIRAZ

Kiraz was born in Cairo to Armenian parents. He attended French schools in Egypt and worked as an illustrator there for three years. In 1946 he took the first boat headed for Paris, where he now lives. His advertisements for Canderel have won awards for best publicity, best posters and the woman's choice from the Syndicat de publicité and *Cosmopolitan*. Kiraz is self-trained as an illustrator and painter. His paintings have been exhibited at Galerie Barlier in Paris. Ten books of Kiraz's illustrations have been published since 1953. The most recent, *Les Parisiennes se marient* (Editions Assouline) was published in 1994.

For thirty years Kiraz made weekly illustrations for *Jours de France* and he currently illustrates a weekly page for *Gala* magazine. His work has also appeared in *Glamour*, *Paris Vogue* and *Playboy*. Among his corporate clients are Nivea and Canderel.

CONTACT:
F: (33) (0)(1) 42 22 14 20

ANJA KROENCKE

Anja Kroencke was born in Vienna in 1968. She studied fashion design and illustration at the College for Textile Design there, graduating in 1987. Kroencke worked as an art director at a large advertising agency in Austria before moving to New York in 1994. Once in New York, she worked as a design director. In 1997 Kroencke began to work full-time as an illustrator. She received a Silver Award from the Society of Newspaper Design in 1997 for her cover illustration for *The New York Times Style Section*. In 1999 she was given the Silver Award by the Creative Club Austria, two Merit Awards and three Distinctive Awards from the Art Director's Club, New York.

Kroencke's work has appeared in *Allure*, German *Elle*, *Madame Figaro*, German and US editions of *Marie Claire*, *The New Yorker*, *The New York Times*, *Travel & Leisure*, *Wallpaper**, *W* and American and Japanese editions of *Vogue*. Her corporate clients include Ann Taylor, British Airways, Estée Lauder, Isetan, Mattel, Motorola, New York City Opera, Polygram, Le Printemps, Ritzenhoff Crystal, Simon & Schuster and Tiffany Japan.

CONTACT (USA):
Kate Larkworthy Artist Representation, Ltd, 80 Nassau Street, 202 East, New York, NY 10038
T: (1) (212) 964 9141
F: (1) (212) 964 9186
e-mail: kate@larkworthy.com

CONTACT (FRANCE):
Prima Linea, 52, boulevard Montparnasse, 75015 Paris
T: (33) (0)(1) 53 63 23 00
F: (33) (0)(1) 53 63 23 01
e-mail: agency@primalinea.com

CONTACT (JAPAN):
Taiko & Associates, 202, 4-3-26 Komaba, Meguro-ku, Tokyo 153 0041
T: (81) (0)(3) 5790 2334
F: (81) (0)(3) 5790 2335
e-mail: hi-taiko@yb3.so-net.ne.jp

JORDI LABANDA

Jordi Labanda was born in Uruguay in 1968 and moved to Barcelona at the age of three. He studied industrial design at the Massana School of Art and Design in Barcelona. Labanda began working as an illustrator in 1994.

Labanda's work has appeared in prominent Spanish publications such as *La Vanguardia*, *El País*, *Elle*, *Woman* and *Vogue*. His work has also appeared in *Amica*, *Allure*, *Cosmopolitan*, *Details*, *Interview*, *Joyce*, *Elle*, *Mademoiselle*, *Marie Claire*, *The New York Times Magazine*, *New York Magazine*, *Süddeutsche Zeitung*, *Visionaire* and *Wallpaper**. Among Labanda's corporate clients are Abercrombie & Fitch, American Express, Citibank, Covergirl, Eurostar, Geffen Records, Hard Rock Hotel & Casino, Knoll International, Microsoft, Neiman Marcus, Pepsi and Ban de Soleil. Some of Labanda's illustrations have been animated for television commercials.

CONTACT (USA):
Art Department, 48 Greene Street, New York, NY 10013
T: (1) (212) 925 4222
F: (1) (212) 925 4422
e-mail: artdept@panix.com

CONTACT (UK):
Art Department, 113 Canalot Studios, 222 Kensal Road, London W10 5BN
T: (44) (020) 8968 8881
F: (44) (020) 8968 8801
e-mail: lucy@artdept-london.co.uk
website: www.art-dept.com

MAXINE LAW

Maxine Law was born in London in 1967. She received a Foundation Diploma from the Central School of Art & Design in 1987 and earned BA with honours and an MA degree, both in graphic design, from Central St Martins. Law currently works at the design firm Aboud•Sodano in London. In 1996 she was nominated for the Creative Future Award.

Her illustrations have appeared in *Flaunt*, *Jane*, *Living Etc.*, *Esquire*, *George*, *Sky* and *Süddeutsche Zeitung Magazin*. Law's corporate work with Aboud•Sodano includes Paul Smith, among other retail and music clients.

CONTACT:
Studio 7, 10–11 Archer Street, Soho, London W1V 7HG
T: (44) (020) 7734 2760/(020) 8621 7974
F: (44) (020) 7734 3551
e-mail: max@aboud-sodano.com

TANYA LING

Tanya Ling was born in India, and grew up in Africa, the USA and England. She graduated with a degree in fashion design from St Martins in 1989. After graduation she moved to Paris to work for Christian Lacroix and Dorothée Bis. Ling's work has been widely exhibited in group and solo shows, including 'The Cover Girl Show' at A22 Projects Gallery in 1998. Ling's artwork was included in the *Pulp Fashion* sale at Sotheby's. She lives in London with her art dealer husband and three children.

Ling's work has appeared editorially in *Elle*, *Frank*, *Harper's Bazaar*, *Nylon* and *Zoo*, British and Japanese editions of *Vogue* and *Joyce*, for whom she illustrated a cover. Additionally, Ling illustrated several trend reports for *Elle* (USA). Her corporate clients include Alfa Romeo, Harrods, Jil Sander and J&M Davidson.

CONTACT:
Bipasha Ghosh/William Ling Fine Art, 30 Gap Road, London SW19 8JG
T+F: (44) (020) 8543 6731
e-mail: william.ling@btinternet.com

LORENZO MATTOTTI

PIET PARIS

THIERRY PEREZ

Lorenzo Mattotti was born in 1954 in Brescia, Italy. He trained as an architect in Venice, and later started to work as a comics and fashion illustrator. In 1995 an exhibition devoted to his work was held in Rome at the Palazzo delle Esposizioni. He has illustrated numerous children's and comic books, including *Fuochi*, which has won many awards. Mattotti's work has appeared in advertising campaigns and on the covers of *Le Monde, The New Yorker* and *Süddeutsche Zeitung*. He lives in Paris with his family.

Mattotti's work has appeared in *Cosmopolitan, Courrier International, Le Monde, Le Nouvel Observateur, Libération, The New Yorker, Süddeutsche Zeitung, Sourrier International, Telerama, Vanity* and *Deutsche Vogue*, among other publications. His corporate clients include Aperol, Kenzo, Le Printemps, Mairie de Paris, Renault and Veuve Cliquot.

CONTACT:
Prima Linea, 52, boulevard Montparnasse, 75015 Paris
T: (33) (0)(1) 53 63 23 00
F: (33) (0)(1) 53 63 23 01
e-mail: agency@primalinea.com

Born in The Hague, Piet Paris currently lives along a canal in Amsterdam. Paris received a BA from the Academy of Fine Arts in Arnhem, where he studied painting as well as fashion design and illustration. Paris has had several solo exhibitions in Amsterdam and his illustrations appear in *Fashion for Fat Women* (Cantecleer, 1990) and *(Hand)bags: A Lexicon of Style* (Rizzoli, 2000) (UK title, *Bags*, 1999).

Paris's work has appeared in Dutch *Cosmopolitan, Elle* and *Marie Claire*, as well as in *American Salon, Chiq,Composite/Japan, Dutch, Hi Fashion Japan, Man Magazine* and *Russian Cult*. He also covers fashion for *De Telegraaf*, the daily newspaper. Among Paris's corporate clients are Amici, Elektra Records, Estée Lauder, Gasunie, Gem Kingdom, Georgette Koning, MAC Cosmetics, Oililly, Peek & Cloppenburg and Studio Edelkoort.

CONTACT (USA):
UNIT NYC, 125 Cedar Street, 2N, New York, NY 10006
T: (1) (212) 766 4117
F: (1) (212) 766 4227

CONTACT (EUROPE):
UNIT CMA, Egelantiersstraat 143, 1015 ra Amsterdam
T: (31) (0) (20) 530 6000
F: (31) (0) (20) 530 6001
website: www.unit_amsterdam.com

Thierry Perez was born in 1964 in Tarbes, France. He studied at L'Ecole Supérieure d'Art Moderne. Perez began his career as an illustrator working with Jean-Paul Gaultier, drawing the collections. He also collaborated with Azzedine Alaïa and Gianni Versace. Most recently he has worked with Pascal Humbert and Jeremy Scott. Currently, Perez is happily living in Paris with his "G3 MAC girlfriend" and working on animated shorts for a production company.

Perez's work has appeared in *Elle, Glamour, Visionaire* and *Vogue Italia*.

CONTACT (FRANCE):
Michele Filomeno, 9, rue de la Paix, 75002 Paris
Contact: Oliver
T: (33) (0)(1) 55 35 35 00
F: (33) (0)(1) 55 35 08 80
e-mail: oliver@mfilomeno.com
website: www.mfilomeno.com

CONTACT (USA):
Michele Filomeno USA Corp., 155 Spring Street, New York, NY 10012
T: (1) (212) 965 1000
F: (1) (212) 965 0869
e-mail: ziggy@mfilomeno.com
website: www.mfilomeno.com

DEMETRIOS PSILLOS

GRAHAM ROUNTHWAITE

KRISTIAN RUSSELL

Demetrios Psillos was born in London in 1967 to Greek Cypriot parents. He received a BA with honours in fashion from Middlesex Polytechnic. Psillos worked with John Galliano for three seasons before he began a career as an illustrator. Soon after he moved to New York. After living there for four years, he returned to London, where he is currently based.

Psillos's work has appeared in British *Vogue, Harper's Bazaar, The New Yorker, Travel & Leisure, Town & Country* and *Wallpaper**. Among his corporate clients are Barneys New York, Bergdorf Goodman, Bloomingdale's, Macy's, Octopus and Ritzenhoff Cristal.

CONTACT:
17F Clerkenwell Road, London EC1M 5RD
T: (44) (020) 7250 1344
F: (44) (020) 7490 1175

Graham Rounthwaite was born and lives in London. He received a BA with honours in graphic design from the Chelsea School of Art, and completed a Masters degree in Illustration at the Royal College of Art. From 1996 to 1998 Rounthwaite was the Art Director of *Trace Magazine*. He works as a designer at *The Face* magazine.

Rounthwaite's work has appeared editorially in *The Face, Details, Elle, Raygun, The Guardian* and *The Telegraph*. His corporate clients include Levi's silverTab® (USA), Fabergé (UK), National AIDS Awareness (France), God's Love AIDS Charity (USA), Top Shop and Carhartt. Additionally, he has worked with many record companies, including Concrete and Creation Records, RCA, EMI and Virgin. He has worked for publishing firms such as HarperCollins and Orion, as well as for TV and video clients, including MTV Europe, Avex UK and Partizan.

CONTACT (USA):
Art Department, 48 Greene Street, New York, NY 10013
T: (1) (212) 925 4222
F: (1) (212) 925 4422
e-mail: artdept@panix.com

CONTACT (UK):
Art Department, 113 Canalot Studios, 222 Kensal Road, London W10 5BN
T: (44) (020) 8968 8881
F: (44) (020) 8968 8801
e-mail: lucy@artdept-london.co.uk
website: www.art-dept.com

Kristian Russell was born in Stockholm in 1968 and grew up between London and Sweden. He completed a foundation course in art and design at Brighton and studied the history of art and design at Staffordshire Polytechnic. Russell began working as an illustrator in 1995. His work has been exhibited in Sweden and he has published two books, one on rave culture. In 1997 Russell designed a series of snowboards for TNT. Russell is based in Stockholm, where he is heavily involved in the music scene. He is the art director of Revolver, a production company based in the Royal Opera House.

Russell's work has appeared in many publications, including *Arena, Bibel, Dazed & Confused, Frank, George, Jane, Mademoiselle, Nylon, Scene, Spin, Sunday Telegraph* and *Svenska Dagbladet (City)*. His has also worked with corporate clients, such as Add (n) to X, Boudicca, Coca-Cola, Diesel Sweden, Elektra, ESPN, Maharishi, RCA, Saatchi & Saatchi, Seagrams, Time Warner, Tie Rack, Tommy Boy, Vexed Generation and Warner Brother Records.

CONTACT (USA):
Art Department, 48 Greene Street, New York, NY 10010
T: (1) (212) 925 4222
F: (1) (212) 925 4422
e-mail: artdept@panix.com

CONTACT (UK):
Art Department, 113 Canalot Studios, 222 Kensal Road, London W10 5BN
T: (44) (020) 8968 8881
F: (44) (020) 8968 8801
e-mail: lucy@artdept-london.co.uk
website: www.art-dept.com

HIROSHI TANABE

Hiroshi Tanabe was born in Kanagawa, Japan in 1967. He graduated from Tama Art College with a degree in graphic design and later studied fine art and sculpture at the Accademia di Brera in Milan. Tanabe was awarded the British *Vogue*/Sotheby's Cecil Beaton Award for fashion illustration in 1994. Tanabe's work has been internationally exhibited. In 1998 he had a show in Japan at Parco Gallery with Jeffrey Fulvimari. A book of his work, *Blue Mode,* was published by Korinsha in 1998 and it won a gold medal for illustration and design from The Art Director's Club in 1999. In 1997 Tanabe designed a line of mannequins for Pucci International. Tanabe lives between Japan and New York City.

Tanabe works regularly for a number of Japanese publications. His work has also appeared in *Arena*, British and Japanese editions of *Vogue*, *Harper's Bazaar*, German *Marie Claire*, *New York Magazine*, *The New York Times*, *The New Yorker*, *Rolling Stone*, *Visionaire* and *Wallpaper**. His corporate clients include Ann Taylor, Anna Sui, Barneys New York, Elektra Records, HBO, Redken and Shiseido.

CONTACT (USA):
Kate Larkworthy Artist Representation, Ltd, 80 Nassau Street, 202 East, New York, NY 10038
T: (1) (212) 964 9141
F: (1) (212) 964 9186
e-mail: kate@larkworthy.com

CONTACT (JAPAN):
A.K.A. Management, 4-23-14, 6th Floor, Ebisu, Shibuya-ku, Tokyo, 150-0013
T: (81) (0)(3) 5423 0033
F: (81) (0)(3) 5423 0036

RUBEN TOLEDO

Ruben Toledo was born in Cuba in 1961. Toledo studied at the School of Visual Arts in New York. In 1984 he married Isabel, a designer, with whom he works in New York City. Toledo paints, sculpts, and designs visual displays, murals and theatrical productions, in addition to working as an illustrator. He has designed sixteen lines of mannequins. Toledo's work has been exhibited in numerous solo and group exhibitions in galleries and museums around the world, including The Louvre and The Metropolitan Museum of Art. His art and collaboration with Isabel is featured in *Toledo/Toledo: A Marriage of Fashion and Art* (Korinsha, 1997). Toledo has also illustrated numerous catalogues and in 1996 he published his own book, *The Style Dictionary* (Abbeville), which has been followed by *Toledo's New York Scrapbook*, published by Louis Vuitton in 1998.

Toledo's work has appeared in many publications, including *Harper's Bazaar*, *Interview*, *L'Uomo Vogue*, *Details*, *Paper*, *Town & Country*, *Visionaire*, and American and German editions of *Vogue*. Among Toledo's corporate clients are Barneys New York, Bergdorf Goodman, Ian Schrager Hotels, Louis Vuitton, Saks Fifth Avenue, Seibu Department Store and VH1.

CONTACT:
F: (1) (212) 685 1578

Ed. TSUWAKI

Ed. Tsuwaki was born in 1966 in Hiroshima. A self-trained artist, Tsuwaki moved to Tokyo after graduation from high school and worked as a typographer and art director. A painter, Tsuwaki also worked on stage sets and did live painting and body painting sessions with music. His first exhibition of paintings was held in 1994. Tsuwaki's experimentation in the field of painting led him to his current method of working on the computer and his career as an illustrator.

Tsuwaki's work has appeared in *Citizen K International*, *Vogue Nippon* and *Wallpaper**. Among his corporate clients are Angel & Blue, Anna Sui, Keita Maruyama and Omega.

CONTACT (JAPAN):
Hiruta Management Office, Tokyo
T: (81) (0)(3) 5405 9486
F: (81) (0)(3) 5405 9487
e-mail: c_hiruta@msn.com

CONTACT (USA):
Art Department, 48 Greene Street, New York, NY 10013
T: (1) (212) 925 4222
F: (1) (212) 925 4422
e-mail: artdept@panix.com

CONTACT (UK):
Art Department, 113 Canalot Studios, 222 Kensal Road, London W10 5BN
T: (44) (020) 8968 8881
F: (44) (020) 8968 8801
e-mail: lucy@artdept-london.co.uk
website: www.art-dept.com

MAURICE VELLEKOOP

Maurice Vellekoop was born in Toronto and now lives on Toronto Island with his cat. Vellekoop attended Ontario College of Art and graduated in 1986. He then joined Reactor agency and began his career as an illustrator. Two books of his work have been published, *Maurice Vellekoop's ABC Book* (Gates of Heck, 1998) and *Vellevision* (Drawn & Quarterly, 1998). Among the books he has illustrated is *Sex Tips from a Dominatrix* (Regan Books, 1999).

Vellekoop's work has appeared in *Cosmopolitan, GQ, Mademoiselle, Männer Vogue, The New York Times Magazine* and *Wallpaper**. He illustrates a monthly column for *Vogue*. Among his corporate clients are Abercrombie & Fitch, Air Canada, Bush Irish Whiskey UK and Swissair.

CONTACT:
Reactor, 51 Camden Street, Toronto, Ontario, M5V 1V2
T: (1) (416) 703 1913
F: (1) (416) 703 6556
e-mail: isousa@reactor.ca
website: www.reactor.ca

LISELOTTE WATKINS

Liselotte Watkins was born in Sweden in 1971. She studied advertising and illustration at The Art Institute of Dallas and returned to Sweden after graduation. In 1994 she went to New York on an extended vacation and immediately landed a weekly commission with Barneys New York, which lasted for two years. After living in New York for several years, she moved back to Stockholm.

Watkins' editorial work has appeared in *Bibel, Elle, Frank, GQ* (Australia), *Marie Claire, The New York Times, Self, Travel & Leisure, Wallpaper** and *Vogue*, as well as on covers of *Amica* magazine. Her corporate clients include American Movie Classics, Anna Sui, Barneys New York, Bergdorf Goodman, Estée Lauder, Grey Advertising, MTV, Ogilvy & Mather, Screaming Mimi's, Simon & Schuster, Sony, Target and Victoria's Secret.

CONTACT (USA):
UNIT NYC, 125 Cedar Street, 2N, New York, NY 10006
T: (1) (212) 766 4117
F: (1) (212) 766 4227

CONTACT (EUROPE):
UNIT CMA, Egelantiersstraat 143, 1015 ra Amsterdam
T: (31) (0)(20) 530 6000
F: (31) (0)(20)530 6001
website: www.unit_amsterdam.com

ACKNOWLEDGMENTS

The author extends heartfelt thanks to the following people:

ARTISTS
Ruben Alterio, Robert Clyde Anderson, François Berthoud, Jason Brooks, Amy Davis, Jean-Philippe Delhomme, Carlotta, Michael Economy, Jeffrey Fulvimari, Tobie Giddio, Mats Gustafson, Yoko Ikeno, Kareem Iliya, Kiraz, Anja Kroencke, Jordi Labanda, Maxine Law, Tanya Ling, Lorenzo Mattotti, Piet Paris, Thierry Perez, Demetrios Psillos, Graham Rounthwaite, Kristian Russell, Hiroshi Tanabe, Ruben Toledo, Ed. Tsuwaki, Maurice Vellekoop, Liselotte Watkins

AGENTS AND PUBLICATIONS
Sylvie Flaure at 2e Bureau, Heloise Goodman at Art & Commerce, Lucy Bone, Marty Byrd, Stephanie Pesakoff and Taisa Skulsky at Art Department, Christine Carter, Adamo DiGregorio and Amy Raiter at Barneys New York, Joelle Chariau at Bartsch & Chariau, William Ling at Bipasha Ghosh/William Ling Fine Art, Carole Glass, Keiko Hidaka, Keiko Nakano, Caroline Stone and Junko Wong at CWC International, Hiruta Chie at Hiruta Management, Julie Hughes at *Joyce* (Hong Kong), Rocco Bonavita, Claribel Corona and Kate Larkworthy at Kate Larkworthy Artist Representation, Gay Feldman and Jay Sternberg at Kramer & Kramer, Albert at *Manhattan File*, Scott Ashwell at *Paper*, Donald Schneider at *Paris Vogue*, Valerie Busenaro at Philippe Arnaud, Bruno Semerarot at PMI, Valerie Schermann and Valérie Lagriffoul at Prima Linea, Isabel Sousa at Reactor Art & Design, KK Davis and John Kiladis at TWBA Chiat Day, Jasper Bode and Tim Groen at Unit CMA, Richard Spenser Powell at *Wallpaper**, Thierry Kaufmann and Srenica Morisot at Yannick Morisot

COLLEAGUES, FRIENDS AND FAMILY
Igor Astrologo, Anne Barlow, Hedwige Caldairou, Susan Cianciolo, Marlene Gamage, Ronnie Davidson-Houston, Helen Farr, Tara Ferri, Dean Kaufman, Tiggy Maconachie, Rina Mattotti, Olivier North, Anna Perotti, Luca Pizzaroni, Miyuki Morimoto, John Sahag, Don Sipley, Valerie Steele, Isabel Toledo, Kirsten Ulve, Michael Washburn and especially Mr and Mrs Matthew Borrelli, M. Carter Borrelli, Mr and Mrs Donald B. Himes, Johanna Neurath, Niki Medlik and Jamie Camplin.